Life on the Farm & Ranch

South Dakota Stories

Edited by
John E. Miller

South Dakota Humanities Council
Brookings, South Dakota

Library of Congress Cataloging in Publication Data

Miller, John E.
South Dakota Stories

John E. Miller

1. South Dakota - Biography
2. South Dakota - History.
3. Agriculture - South Dakota - History.
4. Farm Life - South Dakota - History.
5. Ranch Life - South Dakota - History.

0-9632157-8-7

First Edition
Manufactured in the United States of America
by Mailway Printers

Compiled and Edited by John E. Miller
Text and Transcription: Virginia Harrington
Design and Layout: Cindy Stande

Front Cover Photography: Greg Latza, Used with permission by Greg Latza.
Back Cover Photography: Jean Laughton, Used with permission by Jean Laughton.
Front & Back Inside Covers: Photo Courtesy of the State Archives of the South Dakota State Historical Society.

ii

PEOPLE ARE SAYING...

"The time-honored fashion of delivering history by storytelling is still alive in South Dakota. Our memories provide a simple learning tool about what makes life on the prairie so special and fascinating, and we should continue to pass our stories down to future generations. I remember picking rocks. I remember fixing fences, calving season, and going out to get cattle that got loose in the middle of the night."

South Dakota Governor Mike Rounds, Pierre

"Growing up on my family's fourth generation farm and ranch near Houghton, I cherished our rural way of life and I'm grateful the South Dakota Humanities Council has set about collecting stories of those who have played a critical role in shaping our state's unique heritage. This invaluable contribution preserves the story of our state by collecting the stories of an experience shared by so many South Dakotans. Life on the farm and ranch also helps us to understand how we arrived where we are today and contemplate the possibilities for tomorrow."

Representative Stephanie Herseth Sandlin, Brookings

"I've been in fancy glass offices in Rapid City and Sioux Falls and often heard conversations turn to the price of wheat in Aberdeen or the adventure of branding calves in Dewey County. Many of our top executives and leaders look out from their desks on a summer day and wish they could spend the afternoon on a horse or tractor. We've become more urbane along with the rest of the United States, but our farm and ranch culture is deeply embedded in the soul of South Dakota. Stories of the land and the men and women who love it are both entertaining and enlightening because they introduce us to ourselves."

Bernie Hunhoff, Publisher of "South Dakota Magazine," Yankton

"To me, this book describes how education and an agricultural upbringing form the perfect marriage. An agricultural background instills an unequaled work ethic in our citizens, develops an appreciation of nature and formulates the value of neighbors and friendships while education opens the door to the future where you are limited by your dreams."

Terry Baloun, South Dakota Board of Regents, Sioux Falls

"With roots planted four generations deep in South Dakota's farm and ranch heritage, I know you will enjoy these inspiring stories that encapsulate and forever preserve our state's heritage. As you read them, you will laugh, cry, sympathize, and remember what an honor it is to call South Dakota home. Enjoy!"

Representative Kristi Noem, Farmer/Rancher, Castlewood

"My father worked with farmers and ranchers all his life as a Farmers Home Administration Supervisor—two quotes that I remember: "Don't lend them too much & don't lend them too little" also 'diversify, diversify'."

Bill Walsh, Owner of Dakota Travel, Deadwood

"There is no better way to chronicle change than through those who live it, as seen in Life on the Farm and Ranch. Not only is it interesting to descendants and bystanders, it is important for the historians that monitor agriculture, civilization's oldest and most important industry."

Matt Sutton, Retired Rancher & Sutton Bay Golf, LLC Partner, Agar

"There is nothing more American than the stories of South Dakota farm and ranches. A book that gathers those stories is a document for all times. In these pages, you will find most of what really matters in the lives of all Americans."

Dan O'Brien, Rancher & Author, Hermosa

"South Dakota's farming heritage is an integral part of our state's culture and history. Today's farmers and ranchers are a living link to our state's past and a bridge to our future as well. Growing up in Murdo I had the chance to learn firsthand the lessons and joys of growing up and living in a rural area. This collection of stories can connect future generations of South Dakotans with those that went before, preserving the richness of our heritage for years to come."

U.S. Senator John Thune, Sioux Falls

"These glimpses into real life share tales of admirable qualities of resourcefulness, stamina and determination that are commonplace in rural South Dakota. Pulling them together in such a volume provides a wonderful lesson in life detailing the values held by my parents and grandparents and ones that I treasure. Many will be able to identify with the stories that could come directly from their own lives."

Connie Sieh Groop, Farm Forum Editor, "Aberdeen American News," Frederick

"I have had a life time love affair with the Farm families of South Dakota not because they tended to support me in my elections, but because they are at the very heart of this great State that we all love."

Senator George McGovern, Mitchell

"The stories in this impressive collection demonstrate how foundational good storytelling is to understanding human history and the evolution of the human spirit."

Charles Woodard, SDSU Distinguished Prof. of English, Brookings

"I have lived on a ranch most of life. I grew up on a ranch on Corn Creek in what was then Washabaugh (now Jackson) County. These stories bring to mind so many of my life experiences. I am so glad that someone took the time to capture these wonderful times!"

Elsie M. Meeks, State Director, USDA Rural Development, Huron

EXCERPTS FROM
LIFE ON THE FARM & RANCH

THE YEAR OF 1968-69, while Dad was living on a farm southeast of Wakonda, it began snowing the weekend after Thanksgiving and continued every weekend for weeks, until drifts reached the height of twenty feet. Snow plows quit trying to keep the roads open. School was held for students who could reach the paved roads. His children walked a mile one way to meet the school bus on the blacktop south of the farm.

Gloria Bauske

AS A FARMWIFE, I consider it very important to host daily business luncheons over the noon hour. Now my clientele do not wear three-piece suits, not even leisure suits. It's "casual Friday" everyday here. Instead of Wall Street Armani duds, they sport denim jeans and layer shirts that may have seen their better day, with hooded sweatshirts displaying seed corn or livestock pharmaceutical logos. Don't let their attire fool you. They are definitely businessmen, and business is definitely discussed.

Karla Pazour

THE TRIBE STARTED A CATTLE PROGRAM called the Repayment In-Kind Program, which gave cattle to tribal members. The idea was to get the tribal members to become cattle ranchers. No money was involved with this program. Prior to 1934, every Cheyenne River Sioux Tribal member received 160 acres of land, called allotment land. The rest of the land was controlled by the BIA area office in Aberdeen.

Harlan Gunville, Sr.

ACKNOWLEDGEMENTS

THE SOUTH DAKOTA HUMANITIES COUNCIL wishes to express its gratitude to John Miller for his dedication and book editing, Virginia Harrington for her text processing efforts, LaVerne Rens and Doris Giago of the SDHC Book Committee, and Cindy Strande, SDSU graphic design intern, for her design and layout of the book.

With appreciation, thank you to those who contributed to the text, photograph, technical, and research assistance:

Sherry DeBoer, Stephanie Horsley, and Jay Willms (Council staff members), The South Dakota Agricultural Heritage Museum in Brookings, SD, South Dakota State Historical Archives, Michael Anderson, Charmaign Roisum Aronson, Helen Sederstrom Barney, Gloria Bauske, Andrea Beyers, Linda Gloe Bornitz, Pat Breidenbach, Ruth Buchmann, Kathryn Stenghor Callies, John T. Capone, Chuck Cecil, Jan Cerney, James Cissell, Heather Collins, Lorraine Collins, Elizabeth Cook-Lynn, Marian Cramer, William R. Cutts, Sr., Adrienne DeBoer, Wyatt DeJong, Ronald Dufek, Harvey DuMarce, Suzanne England, Grant J. Fifield, Marie Giago, Robert F. Gloe, Jane Green, Harlan Gunville, Sr., Lillian Hand, Phyllis Hanson, Mary Alice Haug, Anglea I. Henriksen, Greg Latza, Jean Laughton, Onalee Lytle Hoffman, Craig Howe, Betty Jo Huff, Fee Jacobsen, Verlyss V. Jacobson, David Jones, Irean Jordan, Dewayne Kangas, Ronald Kangas, Jeanne Kirsch, Marilyn Kratz, Norma Kruger, Anne LaBrake, Elden Lawrence, Claudia Little, Lil Manthei, Naida McKinney, Eleanore Rowan Moe, Rosemary Dunn Moeller, Gerald Mohatt, Denton E. Morrison, Kathleen Nagel, Nathan Nagel, Jerry Nelson, Micaela Nelson, Berthetta Ness, Louis Niehus, decd., Winfred Noem, Larry Noem, Paula Ness Northrup, Kim Ode, Joran Olson, Melba Olverson, Karla

Pazour, Millie Petersen, Karla Rawden Pritchard, Adelbert Rawden, Doreen Ronning, Bruce Roseland, Carol Roush, Peggy Sanders, Billee Schaible, Barbara Schnell, Vonnie Shields, Kay Smeenk, Daniel G. Snethen, Sonja Stormo, Della Studt, Norman Thomsen, Chester VanderZee, Helena VanderZee, decd., Dorothy Edwards Weinberger, Lisa Apland Wells, Barbara A. White, Courtney Huse Wika, and Ruby R. Wilson.

By Jean Laughton, Used with permission by Jean Laughton.

CONTENTS

Photo courtesy of the State Archives of the South Dakota State Historical Society.

INTRODUCTION

NO SINGLE FACTOR has been more important in influencing the history of the area that we know today as South Dakota than agriculture. The first people on the land, the American Indians, depended initially upon hunting and gathering, then upon agriculture, supplemented by trade, and finally upon following the buffalo. When European settlers arrived during the 1800s, they, too, depended for many decades upon a primarily agricultural way.

The great Columbia University historian Richard Hofstadter began one of his Pulitzer Prize-winning books with this arresting sentence: "The United States was born in the country and has moved to the city." That can stand as a summary of the American historical adventure. The South Dakota story shares in this grand narrative, but from the beginning of white settlement to the present, the area was and remains more agricultural than the rest of the country. From a peak of approximately 83,000 farms and ranches in the middle of the Great Depression, the number has steadily declined to around 30,000 as we end the first decade of the twenty-first century. Yet, the number of acres being utilized by farmers and ranchers has remained relatively stable for decades.

The shift in the United States from the country to the city, and the transition from an agricultural way of life to one dominated by cities and industry entail many contradictions. Economic productivity and output have expanded exponentially both on the farm and ranch and in city workplaces and emporiums. Our standard of living has doubled every generation or so. We Americans are, over all, healthier, longer-lived, better-housed and clothed, more comfortable, and increasingly supported by all manner of technological innovations and machine-made goods. On the other hand, we are more worried about the future. Relative wealth and comfort seem to have brought us no permanent increase in satisfaction, sense of accomplishment, or happiness. A large majority of Americans assert that they would prefer to live in small towns and rural areas even as they inexorably drive up the population of the metropolis, clog its roadways, pollute its environment, and attempt to navigate the rat race.

Life on South Dakota's farms and ranches by no means constitutes a utopia, nor has it done so. But living there confers its compensations, why else would so many people enjoy telling the kinds of stories collected in this volume? South Dakota residents are like their counterparts in every time and place: bundles of contradictions—a little lower than the angels, on the one hand, and scamps, gossips, and busybodies, on the other. But the advantages of living on the land are many: communion with nature, human scale, connection with neighbors, physical exertion, a sense of accomplishment, and closeness to the infinite.

The story of South Dakota agriculture has been one of continual advances in technology replacing human labor. Thus, what may appear at first glance to be a story of decline and failure, looked at from a different vantage point becomes one of progress and triumph. Fewer workers today produce much larger outputs of agricultural products than ever before. Ultimately, we need to ask ourselves what impact improvements in technology, farming techniques, and business practices have upon the daily lives of the people living on farms and ranches and on the people living in the towns and cities that remain dependant upon them. Along with that, what are the qualities and characteristics that make for the good way of life?

The stories contained in this volume touch only sparingly upon the remarkable technological improvements and changes in farming methods that have transformed the rural countryside during the past several decades. Instead, they focus, as one might expect, upon the everyday lives of people living on South Dakota ranches and farms and the memories they retain of their immensely variegated experiences from childhood through adulthood. We asked people to send in stories about their lives and experiences in agriculture, and they responded as one might have anticipated they would by telling about the episodes and routines that reverberated most strongly in their minds.

The stories they sent in sorted out rather naturally, but also to some extent arbitrarily, into the twelve sections that make up this book. In many instances, I could have placed a particular story in several different categories and it would have made as much sense. I tried as much as possible to include at least one story sent in by every respondent, but that did not always work out perfectly. For all of those who did not get a story accepted, as well as for those who did (some having two or more), the South Dakota Humanities Council and I offer our sincere and heartfelt thanks. The most frequent reasons for not including a story submitted to us were that we already had one like it, or the particular category it would have fit into was already well-covered. My most frequent reaction in reading the submissions was one of surprise and delight because of my failure to anticipate the kinds of themes and happenings that might be described. I believe that you, the readers, will be equally surprised and delighted, just as you will often nod your heads in recognition at many of the stories that will remind you of similar circumstances in your own lives.

This is the fourth in a series of volumes published by the South Dakota Humanities Council, an affiliate of the National Endowment for the Humanities. After editing three previous volumes on country churches, one-room country schools, and homefront stories, my friend and colleague Chuck Woodard decided to pass the editorial baton over to me for this one. It has been a pleasant and eye-opening experience for me, as I hope that reading it will be for you. I would like to thank Chuck and LaVerne Rens, as well as Sherry DeBoer and Stephanie Horsley of the South Dakota Humanities Council, for all of the fine advice and assistance they gave me. This has truly been a collective effort. With people of this caliber working for the humanities in this state, and readers like you participating in and supporting humanities programs, you can expect more volumes like this one to be produced. We welcome your input and suggestions for what kinds of topics to address.

John E. Miller
Brookings, South Dakota

PRELUDE

Country Chores

A farm was a busy life.
There was always something to do.
I had many indoor chores
And outdoor tasks, too.

I learned to peel pounds of potatoes,
And washing dishes was left for me.
Bushel baskets of ironing piled high
Prevented me from running free.

And off to the potato patch
I took a little pail,
Flicked off potato bugs,
Munching leaves looking quite frail.

Water to pump and carry
To animals about the farm,
Eggs to gather in the coop
And from the manger in the barn.

I fetched cows from the corn stubble.
They fed on ears left behind.
Towards the barn they sauntered,
A job I really didn't mind.

In frosty cold weather,
I hung laundry on the line.
In summer the wind blew like fury,
Around the clothes line it twined.

To ranch duties I still attend,
Remembering chores of long ago.
Thankful for a rural life,
You reap what you sow.

Jan Cerney,
Rural Dixon

Photo courtesy of the State Archives of the South Dakota State Historical Society.

PEOPLE

SD State Agricultural Heritage Museum Photographic Collection.

The Adventures of a Butte County Homesteader

IN THE FALL OF 1909, my grandfather Henry Jacobsen filed on a homestead in north central Butte County (near a butte he would name Castle Rock Butte), and then he returned to his young family in Chicago to prepare for their big adventure to come. The following spring he took the train back from Chicago to Belle Fourche, this time accompanying an "immigrant car" containing his family's possessions and a milkcow purchased with monies from selling his diamond stick pin and his wife's diamond ring.

Upon arrival, Henry discovered that his billfold was missing, surmising it had fallen out of his pocket while shoveling straw and manure out of his immigrant car. Faced with no money, he used his wife's piano as collateral to borrow money in "Belle" to buy building supplies and a team and wagon to "freight" them to his homestead, forty-some miles away. After unloading, he returned to Belle for more lumber. When he returned to his homestead, the first load of lumber was gone! All the questions and comments of his fellow salesmen in Chicago, who thought he was crazy to leave a good job there to homestead in western South Dakota, must have haunted him for a long time.

In spite of the challenges, frustrations, and additional expenses of those first days of homesteading, Henry was not to be defeated in his desire to establish a homestead and make a life for his family on land he could call his own. He had been fending for himself since 1889, when, at age 10, he ran away from home in Hamburg, Germany, joining another "waif" as a stowaway on a ship sailing (unbeknownst to them) to America. They landed at New York in June.

The boys were sent to the Immigrant Farm in Brooklyn, but they ran away to sing and polish shoes on the streets of New York to make money. As a teenager, Henry took a ranch job in Nebraska for a couple of years before opening a "confectionery" store there. His first business led to a job in Chicago as a cigar inspector, after which he became a traveling salesman for a wholesale foods company.

A month after Henry's arrival at his homestead, he was joined by his wife, Mabel, and sons Francis, 4, and Henry, Jr., 2. That fall, he established the Castle Rock Post Office. The next year he opened a country store. He served as postmaster until 1914, when Mabel took over the duties so he could spend his time ranching. Mabel also ran a "Road Ranch," supplying home-cooked meals and clean beds in their home for "freighters" moving supplies to their homesteads farther north.

As payment on a debt, Henry acquired a printing press that he used to publish The Castle Rock Press from 1912 until he sold it in 1928. In May 1917, Henry was appointed a United States Land Commissioner (a position he held until his death), and between 1932 and 1948, he served as a Butte County Commissioner. During those years, he also became a Butte County political figure known as a fearless advocate of good government and fair play.

Through the years, Henry, with his two sons, continued to increase the size of their sheep ranch, which he divided and sold to them when he retired in 1948. Henry, a self-educated man, died in 1952 after a seventy-three-year life journey that had begun in Hamburg, Germany, and ended in a rural American community he had named.

Pat (Jacobsen) Breidenbach,
Butte County

Dakota Farming Traditions

AS A LAKOTA, I DO NOT KNOW MUCH ABOUT FARMING. My ancestors were hunters and gatherers. They roamed the area which included what is now western South Dakota and never led a sedentary life. Our close relatives, the Dakota, on the other hand, became expert farmers and were known for their abundant crops.

I arrived in Sisseton, in the upper eastern part of South Dakota, on a warm July day. The landscape was green, and the corn was weeks away from harvest. I could see why the Dakota people were known for farming as I looked over the landscape so different from Lakota country.

As I approached the Tekakwitha Nursing Home, I was eager to learn about what it was like to be an Indian farmer. While our people are very similar in culture and tradition, our subsistence methods were very different. Francis Crawford is a 100-year-old elder of the Sisseton Wapheton Oyate, and I walked into his room to learn more about Dakota farming. Francis was surrounded by family members. His nephew, Lester Crawford, introduced us. Lester was raised by Francis and is more like his son than his nephew. Francis looked just as I had imagined. He had a warm, inviting smile like many Sioux grandfathers I have known. He has managed to keep his sense of humor over the years and cracked jokes about his knowledge of the Dakota language. Francis grew up speaking Dakota and is still a fluent speaker.

Raised in the Buffalo Lake area of the Lake Traverse Reservation, Francis came from a family of farmers. At a young age Francis, like many Indians during this era, was sent to boarding school. There, he learned the skills he needed to be a successful farmer. Boarding schools had many goals, one of them being to teach useful trades to Indian children in hopes of assimilating them into mainstream society. Francis recalled the many schools he attended and the knowledge he gained.

He first attended Tiospa Zina School on his reservation. He later went to Riggs Institute, now known as the Flandreau Indian School. Lastly, he went to Haskell Indian School in Kansas. Francis reminisced about his daily routine in boarding school. He spent half the day in the classroom and the other half doing chores. "They tried to teach us how to do their kind of work," he said. They rotated chores that ranged from milking the cows to cleaning the dining hall. Milking the cows in the winter could be a difficult job. "It'd be cold, and when you milked, you got up close to the cow cause she was warm, ya know," he said, as we all burst into laughter. The thought of those young boys snuggling up to those cows on a frigid winter morning brought smiles to all of our faces.

While he was attending Haskell Indian School, Francis's mother became very ill. He remembered them calling him into the office to tell him the news and giving him some money to get home. His mother recovered from her illness, but Francis never returned to finish his final year of school.

A short time later, he moved to Oklahoma. The First World War was taking place, and there was a demand for workers. He lived with two of his brothers and found work in the oil fields. "Before I went to Haskell, you didn't get much, no more than a dollar and a half a day or something like that. After I went to work in the oil fields, I can't remember what was paid, but it was a lot more than they paid anywhere else." His job in the oil fields only lasted a few years. Then his parents were moving off the farm, and Francis returned home to take over the land.

Francis recalled the hard times many Indian farmers faced during the Great Depression. They received government rations, but many of them maintained their own gardens. "They (the government) gave out cattle and that's how a lot of Indians got started with cattle," he said. They dried corn and stored potatoes and everyone helped each other. Francis's farm survived the Depression, and he continued to farm for many decades later.

In the Buffalo Lake area, Dakota farmers were not as common as they were in other places on his reservation. Most of Francis's neighbors were Austrian and Norwegian, but he did not recall being treated any different for being Dakota. Farming then was very different than today. "I had good neighbors. They would help me, ya know, my neighbors," he said. Farmers relied heavily on their neighbors throughout the planting and harvesting season. Threshing machines and tractors were expensive and rare. Harvesters would hire Indians and whites to help on their farms. He remembered them as being a community in which people always helped each other.

Francis was well-respected as a farmer. His nephew Lester recalled a conversation he had with a neighbor. The neighbor asked, "Is Francis plowing yet?" Once Francis started plowing, the neighbors knew it was time and followed his lead. When they saw him harvest his crops, they would be harvesting their crops the next day. If Francis bought crop insurance, then they would also purchase some. "I guess they had a sense he knew what the weather was," said Lester. Neighbors relied on his intuition as a farmer and always trusted his judgment.

Farming has changed a lot over the years, but Francis remembers the time when everything they produced went to sustaining their way of life. It was hard work but a good life, he said. Those thoughts stuck in my memory as I returned home. While the techniques, crops, and technology had changed from the days of his ancestors, Francis had still carried their values, and they had influenced him in the sedentary life of a Dakota. He has passed on his traditions and values to Lester, who now farms on the land that generations of Crawfords have farmed before him.

Marie Giago,
Brookings
Story events take place in Buffalo Lake area

County Agent

MY DEAR FRIEND AND COUNTY AGENT, Mel Kloster, passed on a year ago, an anniversary that brought forth a bout of reminiscing. A minor tragedy first caused Mel's path to cross with mine. Our eight-year-old son, who was in his first year of 4-H, decided to show a Holstein heifer calf at Achievement Days. He had spent most of the summer taming the heifer and training her to lead.

We hauled the calf to the county fairgrounds the day before the show. During the night, she somehow managed to garrote herself with her lead rope. We received a call from Mel early the next morning. He told us what had happened and that he had seen to the removal of the deceased animal, sparing our son a very grim surprise.

We later met Mel to retrieve the halter. Mel gently explained to our son that we had done nothing wrong, that these things happen and all we can do is accept them and learn from them and move on. Mel's words helped soften the hard edges of a very harsh situation. I decided right then and there that Mel is a guy I would be glad to call a friend.

I began to consult with Mel on a fairly regular basis. His wit and knowledge of agriculture made each phone call or visit a pleasure. His favorite saying, "Better than a poke in the eye with a sharp stick," had the effect of injecting levity and putting even the most nettlesome situation into perspective.

Mel also helped me navigate the direst straits of my farming career, the morning my cows decided to bloat. We'd had a hot, dry summer and my alfalfa had gone dormant. I was using a rotational grazing system, putting the cattle on a fresh alfalfa paddock each day.

It began to rain about the first of August, continuing until we received several inches. Had I consulted with Mel, I might have known that such conditions can cause alfalfa to break dormancy and put out tender, delicious—and deadly—new growth.

One morning I took the flashlight and the dog and walked out to bring the cows in for milking. Off in the dusky darkness I gradually perceived the outline of an expired bovine, her legs pointing to the sky, her skin taut as a cartoon balloon. Dang it! One of the gals had up and bloated! I chalked it up to extreme bad luck. But then I found another. And another.

Horror. Nausea. Overwhelming panic. I somehow managed to push these aside and trotted the rest of the herd to the barn. Half a dozen cows were thinking seriously about dying, their bellies tight as drumheads. I knew two things. These "bossies" needed to stay on their feet if they were to have any hope of surviving, and I wouldn't be able to accomplish that alone. I ran to the house and made a phone call.

Mel arrived at my farm in a short while. We divided the herd and spent the next couple of hours chasing cows, keeping them on their feet and alive. I am certain that Mel's help saved several head.

We took a breather when things finally seemed under control. Mel lit a cigarette, and the combined aroma of tobacco smoke and cow manure instantly transported me back to my childhood in my parents' dairy barn. I suddenly felt at peace, as if everything was going to be OK.

Jerry Nelson,
Volga

Grandma's Straw Hat

MY DAD OWNED TRADER TOM'S GAMBLES IN ESTELLINE, but I got a taste of farm living when I visited my Grandma, Elnora Sorenson Schnell. When my grandfather died, Grandma left the big house to my uncle, who managed the family farm outside of Lake Preston. She moved to a small house down the road and arranged my visits to save gas. On Thursdays, I'd pay my quarter for the bus ride to the Red Cross swimming lessons in Arlington. On the way I would read comic books and eat Salted Nut Rolls. After my swimming lesson, Grandma would pick me up in her Chrysler "woody," with plastic seat covers that looked like bubble-wrap.

Friday mornings, I'd get up early with Grandma to do chores. I wore shorts and a T-shirt, but Grandma always wore a belted shirtwaist dress. I think she was a little put off by my informality. She made breakfast, then changed her slippers for work shoes in the mud room, slapped an old straw hat over her netted hair, grabbed her gloves, and strode to her huge vegetable garden, with me trotting behind her. As we hoed corn and harvested tomatoes, Grandma told me about vegetables—and how to preserve them. We'd leave the bushel basket of tomatoes in the mudroom for canning later. Then it was on to the crabapple trees in the shelterbelt. She let me eat the windfalls, which were usually pretty sour, as she checked the crabapples for ripeness for future pies and sauces. We'd finish up by the petunia beds bordering the house. Grandma showed me how to pinch off dead blooms. She always talked about growing snapdragons, but she never did. Grandma really liked those petunias.

Then we'd go inside to make lunch for the men in the field— and us, of course. Grandma kept that chore because her daughter-in-law worked in town. Grandma always made a batch of puff-pastry cookies with rock sugar melted on top. She'd pack up sandwiches, potato salad, and puff-pastry cookies and pour ice water and lemonade into plastic gallon thermoses. Then she'd slap the straw hat back on her head, and we'd pack the food into the Chrysler woody. I'd climb onto the bubble wrap, roll down the window, using the silver handle with the "crystal" knob, and "airplane" my hand in the breeze as we bounced over the rutted field to the men who were waiting for us on a flatbed half full of hay bales. I learned about flowers and vegetables, as well as division of labor, from Grandma. On Tuesdays she would take me back to Arlington, with a miniature cereal box filled with puff-pastry cookies to eat on the bus ride home (I wish I could remember what she called those puff-pastry cookies, because they were lots better than Salted Nut Rolls). I loved those weekends.

Grandma died when I was in the seventh grade. The funeral didn't mean much to me—it was more surreal than anything. The fact of Grandma's death didn't become real until my dad brought home her Chrysler woody. In the back seat, sitting on top of the bubble-wrap plastic, was Grandma's straw hat. Always before, if that hat wasn't on Grandma's head, it was hanging in the mudroom—and there it was, on the back seat.

But I remember Grandma and the lessons she left me. I have my own straw hat now—although I don't think I'll ever wear a shirtwaist to work in the garden. Maybe I'll plant some petunias by the house this year. Some snapdragons might be nice . . . but no, I think it'll be petunias.

Barbara Schnell,
Hamlin County

Richard, the New Mail Man

IT WAS JANUARY 1921. The wind had died down and the snow had stopped. The blizzard was over and the temperature dropped quickly. Fifteen-year-old Rich and his horse Babe had remained in town during the storm. Rich had stayed with Mr. Fuller, the rural mailman. Now he was needed to help deliver the mail. After gathering the mail, Mr. Fuller went one direction and Rich went the other.

Rich and Babe traveled over and around the snowdrifts as quickly as possible in the bitter cold. Rich noticed that the country school on the horizon had smoke coming out of the chimney. Suddenly, he had a time-saving idea. He quickly turned in the direction of the school. When he arrived at the school, he tied his horse to the flag pole in the center of the school yard and went in to give the students the mail for each of their families. This was a questionable idea because guidelines for mail carriers stated that the mail was to be delivered to the address that was on the mail. This did not include dropping it off at the school. He thought he could save time, however, so he handed out the mail, warmed his hands, and even had a snack offered to him by the students.

He ran out of the school to return to town. To his dismay, his horse had loosened the reins, abandoned him, and headed to town. This was a great dilemma. It was eight miles to town and two miles to his Uncle Burt's farm. He slowly turned towards his Uncle's farm, dreading every step he took, knowing what would happen when he arrived at the farm. By the time he arrived, Rich was sick with worry and fear that something might have happened to his horse, and he knew he was in for a stern lecture.

Ashamed, he told his Uncle what happened, and in silent disgust Uncle Burt slowly finished milking cows and feeding the rest of the animals. Uncle Burt harnessed the horses to the sled and they headed to town. Aunt Bea had put some heated bricks in the blankets covering his feet. She also gave him a snack to eat on the way to town. She felt sorry for him, and that made Rich feel even worse.

Meanwhile, Mr. Fuller was horrified to realize that the horse had returned to the barn without Rich. He rushed to the barbershop and gathered as many men as possible. The men hurried to put on warm clothing and to saddle horses. They even harnessed some sleds in case of an emergency.

Halfway between town and Uncle Burt's farm the two parties met. Rich did not know if he should be glad or sad as the stern admonishments were finally over. But now he had to face a group of cold men who had come looking for him. Much to his relief, they were not angry, but just glad to see that he was safe.

Rich learned a lesson that day. He would always remember that "short cuts" do not always save time. He was still embarrassed as he told the story to me many years later. This lesson stayed with him for over sixty years as he carried mail, in all kinds of weather, across the prairies of South Dakota.

Joran Olson,
Rosholt

Beans

AUGUST 2, 1990. That was the day Iraq invaded Kuwait. Living on an irrigated farm/ranch near tiny Oral, why would that event matter to me? Well, for starters, prior to 1990, Iraq had been the importer of fifty percent of the United States' edible bean crop. We had beans to harvest and sell. They became worth nothing in the flash of a gun.

That was only the beginning of how a war in the desert so many miles away would affect our family farm and way of life. On our irrigated farm we raise corn, alfalfa hay, cattle—and boys, which are far and away our best crop. Carl was eleven and Neil, eight, when the war started. My husband, Russ, was an officer in the Army Reserves. When my woman's intuition kicked in, I told Russ that he was going to be involved. He scoffed because he was assigned to Fort Riley, Kansas, and it, he pointed out, had Europe as the primary emphasis. I told him fine, but I was going to get all of our family papers together and get prepared military family-wise anyway. Two days later, Russ got the call from a colonel in the Army Reserves and was told he needed to get to his post in Kansas, 650 miles away.

There was hay to put up, fall cattle work to get done, corn to harvest, and the boys, of course, were in school. We ran the farm by phone, checking in nearly every night. Friends stepped in to help when needed. Problems just got handled in the best manner possible. My brother lived near us and he ran the corn harvest. His father-in-law came from California to drive the farm truck back and forth from the combine in the corn field to the grain bin. My dad and other friends and neighbors pitched in as needed, and others offered. At one point, the grain auger broke, repairs were made, and the job went on. The next fall, Russ commented that he didn't remember fixing the auger in the manner in which it was repaired. I told him that it had broken and someone had reconstructed it and that he would probably find several things like that as he worked. Because he could not be here to fix the problems himself, we just didn't tell him about all of the little things that happened. He had enough to worry about as it was, assigned to a mobilization office and sending other people to their duty stations.

For four and a half months, Russ was gone. He remained in Kansas and did not deploy overseas. He returned to the farm the day the air war started, right on time, just like the Pentagon promised. Six days later we started calving.

Peggy Sanders,
Rural Oral
Previously printed in "The Rocky Mountain Fence Post"

Mom's "Insulation" Technique

I WAS RAISED ON A FARM NEAR TUTHILL, SOUTH DAKOTA. My mom, Charlotte Wallingford, was one of the most resourceful and innovative people I ever knew. Of course, farm wives have always benefited from those innate traits. Mom passed away on August 30, 2007. I miss her so very much, but I, too, have benefited immensely from those endearing traits.

It was the Blizzard of 1949 in central South Dakota. Our small farmhouse was drafty and cold, almost shaking in the driving prairie winds. Mom tucked all four of us kids into our bunk beds in the bedroom we shared. Later in the evening, as the fierce South Dakota winds howled, Mom came into the bedroom to check on us. To her dismay, she discovered that the wind-driven snow had sifted into our bedroom through cracks in the wall and around the ill-fitting windows and had settled like a white quilt onto our covers. She tossed and turned all night, trying to figure out a way to "fix" the drafty old house. By morning, with the blizzard still raging outside, Mom had a potential solution to the snowy dilemma.

Mom made her way to the machine shed, got the hand-held weed sprayer, and took it inside. After filling the weed sprayer with water, she ventured outside again to spray the exterior walls and windows of the house with water. Of course, the water froze almost immediately in the sub-zero temperatures. The ice worked as insulation and kept the cracks in the walls and around the windows sealed up. The house remained toasty warm and draft free for the remainder of the blizzard.

How resourceful was that? Mom's philosophy was, "If it works for the Eskimos in Alaska, why won't it work for a farm family in sub-zero South Dakota?" And it did! All four Wallingford children slept in cozy comfort the rest of that extremely cold winter of 1949.

Billee Schaible,
Rural Vetal

Evelyn

Evelyn was born in 1919,
the daughter of two children
born to homesteaders, the daughter
born of World War One,
or the fear of him going to it.
They married when the war was over,
and Evelyn learned in her thirties
how she came to be.
All she remembers of her childhood
is prairie, sun, cattle, and the love
of a family living alone south of the Cheyenne.
She remembers pumping water,
making bread, cooking over cow-chip fires,
reading the Bible by tallow candles.
Evelyn remembers snakes and coyotes,
buffalo and, dimly, Sioux Indians
coming to the ranch looking for food.
That was after a bad winter,
and the Colby family up north
being found frozen in their dugout home.
Those are the things she remembers.
She doesn't remember, or care to tell,
about the days during her marriage.
Somehow, the drunken husband
doesn't find her tongue, although
he may still be in her heart.
He was found dead in the breaks
after tying one on in Wall one cold fall day.
She doesn't talk about raising the two children,
boy and girl, by herself, and how they kept the ranch
and made it something worthwhile.

She won't tell you about being raped by a transient,
nor how she solved that problem.
God knew what happened,
no need for us to hear.
She won't talk about her daughter
running away with the drifter,
or how she took her and her child back
after he ran with another.
She only smiles when asked about her son
and how he took over the ranch with his wife,
and made it prosper more.
You could ask her more,
and she would not tell, either
because her memory fails,
or because her heart says
it is not hers to tell.
What she will not talk about, or even acknowledge,
is our idea that women like Evelyn
made this land work, for better or worse.
She will not say men could not do
what needed to be done by themselves.
The West was won by women,
who stood their ground in silence,
doing what was necessary.
Evelyn has pictures of her family
on her dresser top in the nursing home.
She sits in her wheel chair,
looking out to the prairie beyond,
a smile or frown across her face,
a tear on her cheek now and then,
remembering what we need not know.

David Jones,
Pennington County

Our Farm Hobo

WE ROWANS HAD AN UNUSUAL VISITOR EACH SUMMER for about five years. I shall never forget the first time I met Mr. Smith. I knew jolly old Santa Claus had arrived. He even had a tummy "that shook when he laughed like a bowl full of jelly." Mr. Smith, whom we all treated with the greatest respect, was proud of his profession—a hobo. In the twenties and thirties hobos rode the trains (in empty cars) from one part of the country to another, stopping off wherever and whenever they chose. In Artesian, the Milwaukee Railroad depot agent pretty much ignored the hobos who camped a few rods down the track by the stockyards. If the heavens opened up, sometimes the hobos slept in empty railroad cars. Otherwise, they seemed to prefer sleeping under the open skies. From the end of April through September, wafts of bacon, chicken, or beef cooking over open fires floated to downtown Artesian.

I do not know how Mr. Smith found the Rowan farm the first time, but it is even more puzzling that my parents trusted him as our guest. He was meticulously clean, slept in the hayloft, but ate all his meals with us. Except for gathering the eggs, I cannot remember Mr. Smith ever working. His tales of the many places he had visited intrigued us each evening as the family and hired hands sat out in the yard after the physical chores of the day were done.

Mr. Smith taught me to dream and to imagine a life I didn't have. Since I was without a playmate, I used my imagination. Whenever I skated on the pond formed by the run-off from the well, I was skating at Lake Placid. When I practiced the piano, I was in concert at Carnegie Hall. When I spoke my elocution pieces, I was on WNAX (Guerney's station in Yankton), the only station we could get on the radio. We were privileged to have a radio. However, to listen, we had to wear ear phones. I can remember neighbors huddling around the Atwater Kent with the three head phones we owned.

My imagination also changed my wardrobe from my flour sack dresses to materials of silk, wool, or velvet. Instead of advertising their logo on the 50-pound sacks, the flour companies printed colored designs. Unfortunately, my mother had to find two sacks of flour with the same design, because I was too tall to wear a dress made from only one flour sack. I would imagine myself as a model in these creations.

In addition, country telephone lines were intriguing. Each telephone had its own distinct ring. If nobody answered on the first ring, the person calling had to turn the little black crank again with the prescribed ring. Nothing was automatic. Rubbernecking was a favorite pastime for almost everyone. The telephone operator in each town alerted everyone with ten short rings—for emergencies, fires, catastrophes, or breaking news. The emergency ten shorts announced the kidnapping of Charles Lindbergh's baby boy in 1932. The ten shorts also announced that baby Lindbergh had been found dead.

Life was simple! These were the Depression years. Grasshoppers completely covered the fence posts, huge flies blackened the north side of the buildings, anthrax was rampant among the cattle, grass fires were frequent, and life had many discouragements. In spite of these problems, our home was full of good jokes, no bickering, and constant planning for the future.

Eleanore Rowan Moe,
Artesian

Working Till the End

OLD MAN BESMER WARNED HIM not to buy what they called the "Starvation Ranch," but my dad was determined to own his own place. Elmer Richardson had grown up in a family who rented. Many March 1st's saw them moving to a new house in the area commonly known as the seven-mile strip, located along the Nebraska/South Dakota border and claimed by both states. In the years between Nebraska's statehood in 1867 and the final border agreement in 1895, outlaws made use of the contested land. Stealing horses was a capital offense, but from Horse Thief Dam it was an easy quarter-mile ride to herd the property in question north over the hill to land which, until 1904, was a part of the Great Sioux Nation.

Elmer was born in this area in 1914. His memories of farming went back to a time when he was so small he had to reach up to grasp the plow handles as he walked a mile-long field—down a mile row, up a mile, down a mile again—behind the team of horses pulling the plow.

He graduated from high school in 1933, but with the Great Depression and World War II, his plans to own his own farm were on hold. He worked as a hired hand for a neighbor, then with the Civilian Conservation Corps on various projects, including carving steps in Wind Cave. In April 1941, six months before the attack on Pearl Harbor, he was drafted. Elmer began sending money home to have his father buy a place. The price was steep—ten dollars an acre. "Don't worry about the money," he wrote to his father. "Either I'll keep sending it, or my death benefits will cover it." Elmer returned home in December 1945 to a deep disappointment. His father had not bought the land. "He said he couldn't bear to think of my death buying the place," Elmer said.

And so it was that in 1946, Elmer Richardson stood in a pasture with Bill Besmer and agreed to buy the worst land around.

He married, and his land holdings grew along with his family. He bought land for himself and a farm for his parents, which he bought again when they retired. A generation left their family farms, but their names stayed in the land that Elmer acquired: the Painter place, the Herman place, Drury's, Whitley's, and Horse Thief Dam pasture. He believed in working hard and living according to his own heart. By age 85, Elmer's Starvation Ranch stretched 2,500 acres. His work was his life and he was happiest when fixing fences or feeding bulls. When he drove into a pasture, the cows came running. They knew he brought a treat for them in the back of his pickup, and they would crowd around him, shoving forward to reach it. Elmer scooped most of the corn onto the ground, but always kept a few ears back for hand feeding. When he was 89, he re-sided the shed in the calving pasture, and the following year he shingled it. When he was 91, his summer project was to put in three miles of new fence. Elmer didn't bother with a tractor-mounted auger; he dug each post hole by hand. "I did it the easy way," he said with a grin. "I poured a little water on the ground before I dug each hole."

Elmer Richardson was part of what Tom Brokaw called the Greatest Generation, and his life was defined by work, determination, and two great events—his service to country, which came to an end in 1945, and the farm which he began in 1946.

Barbara A. White,
Gregory County

Last Days of Cornelius Anthonie Van Wyk

THE LATTER PART OF APRIL 1917, Pa Van Wyk sold a horse, and he wished to ride it one last time. It was Saturday, and Mother, watching from the house, saw him slide off and fall. Soon afterward, he came in and said he felt very bad. He had a lot of pain, but worked some yet. At night, he wanted to shave, but he pushed it aside, saying he would wait until morning.

During the night, he awakened Mother because of the intense pain. She called Henry Munneke, their neighbor, and asked him to call a doctor. There was much suffering all night. He asked Mother to pray, which she did on her knees.

The next day Dr. Rodenhuis came. It was decided that they must operate. Dr. File of Geddes performed the operation on Monday evening at home. A telegram was sent to Uncle Will Van Wyk: "OPERATED ON FOR APPENDICITIS NOT EXPECTED TO LIVE."

Tuesday, all the brothers and sisters were called. The bed had been moved into the front room; the head end was raised. Grandma DenBesten was sitting, praying silently. Relatives all passed by for a goodbye kiss. He said, "I've given myself soul and body into the hands of the Lord Jesus. You must all come too. I'm going to Jesus, Mama; are you satisfied to let me go? Soon I will be rejoicing before God's throne with all the holy angels. Grandma DenBensten will likely be the first to come. Cornelius, you must take good care of Mama." Then to the nurse, he said, "If you want to meet Him there, you must serve him here. Do you know our God?"

He watched the sun rise on Tuesday morning and said that he might live until two o'clock. It was at that exact time that he died. Just before his death, because of much discomfort, he asked to sit and then to lie down again. He asked Mother to make some tea, as he wanted to spare her seeing it all. Suddenly he threw up and was gone. The date was May 1, 1917. Cornelius was 40 years old. Margaret continued living on the farm that summer and hired the farm work done.

Helena VanderZee, Deceased
Douglas County
Submitted by Chester VanderZee

KIDS

SD State Agricultural Heritage Museum Photographic Collection.

Girls and Horses

I GREW UP ON THE "ROISUM HOMESTEAD," one mile west of Lake Norden. My two sisters, Donna and Connie, were born in 1929 and 1938, respectively. I was the middle child, born in 1933.

When we were young, we girls were very interested in animals. They were not only a necessity on our farm; they were also our entertainment. Little did we know the effect they would have in our and our families' lives!

Our first "project" was the steer named "Jackie." At an early age, Donna broke him to ride, and as he grew up, he was trained to drive. Donna, Connie, and I would drive him to town with a crate of eggs to sell, take a can of cream to the creamery, and pick up groceries or mail. Our folks even arranged for Jackie to be in some local parades. He became quite a favorite among the people! My sisters and I were never quite sure what actually happened to Jackie. Our parents told us that he was "needed" in a parade in Washington.

To replace our beloved steer, Dad brought home a ponyhorse named "Silver." This was the start of our love of horses. We rode everything on our farm. Dad bought a colt and Donna promptly broke him to ride. A horse named "Cutie" came to board on the farm and Connie adopted her. People started bringing horses to us to train, which is how we ended up with "Kay," one of our favorite horses.

When we were bored with purely basic training, we started teaching the horses tricks. The first was jumping. We would put up jumps all over and made them from anything. The horses were getting pretty good at this, so someone had the great idea of lowering the wire fence so we could just jump in and out of the cow pasture and avoid opening and closing the gate to get the milk cows. Yes, it worked, but a little too well. Because our horses were good jumpers, they would freely jump in and out of the pasture to graze.

Our horse Kay really mastered this trick and she never forgot it. She continued the jumping trick for many years.

Another idea we had was to shoe our own horses. There were plenty of shoes lying around the barn, but no horseshoe nails. However, we did have shingling nails. We succeeded in getting shoes on dad's workhorse, Beauty, but I don't know how long they actually stayed on.

When Donna graduated from high school in 1947, she joined the "White Horse Troupe" in Naper, Nebraska. There she found even more love and a longer career in trick riding and training. When Donna would come home to visit, she would teach Connie and me (and the horses) what she had learned. One of the training sessions was teaching the horses to walk planks. We even had one of Dad's work horses, Beauty, walking a plank.

Donna brought two colts, Rusty and Dusty, from the White Horse Ranch. We trained them to jump, and Donna trained us to "Roman Ride" the two colts. Also, during this time, our dad had two ox yokes, so we trained two teams of cattle to drive. We trained Ferdinann with Clarabelle and Frankie with Johnny.

In 1949, we were asked to put together a show in Estelline. We also put on shows in Lake Preston and Lake Norden. We had jumping routines. Donna would ride "Roman style" over jumps. We also had Ferdinann and Clarabelle standing on pedestals with all four feet, and they could even walk a plank. At the Lake Norden show, while Connie was jumping with Rusty, he straddled the bar and fell. Needless to say, Connie broke both her arms!

In 1950, Connie and I drove the two teams of cattle in the Days of '76 parade. Most exciting was Donna joining a troupe of girls from California called the "Valkeries." I rode with them one year, but Donna continued with them until they disbanded a few years later. In 1951 and 1954, the "Valkeries" performed at Madison Square Garden. One of Donna's featured trick acts was jumping five horses at a time. Donna's favorite trick act was jumping a six-horse tandem. Standing on the back team, Donna would have them circle the arena, then through a figure eight and over a jump.

Donna and Connie are gone now, but these were, and still are, great memories and these memories were always part of the conversation when we got together.

Charmaign Roisum Aronson,
Rural Lake Norden

Life on the Creek

Remembering Grady, Buggs, and Lorenzo

LIFE ON CROW CREEK was a continual adventure. Living at the bottom of Santee Hill, there were horses to ride, chickens to chase, and games to play. With an older brother and two older sisters, something was always going on. Mom set the boundaries and Grandpa reminded us about our responsibilities. My brother came up with the ideas.

"Look," he said one day, "Wouldn't it be great to have a parachute? Think about everything we could do with it."

I agreed, but being six years of age to his ten, I was not so sure about the logistics of such an operation. He was already explaining the basics to me. "We'll take this string and that old sheet and we'll tie it all together."

Before I could ask any questions, he was already starting, showing me how to bunch up a section of the sheet and tie a length of string to it. It didn't take long before he moved on to the next step. "We have to get all the string tied together now and they have to be even," he stated.

I wasn't much help. In fact, I seemed to be getting in the way more than helping. Soon he had the string assembled the way he wanted it. He demonstrated how the material would puff out and explained that was what would make the parachute work. It made sense to me.

It wasn't even lunchtime, so we had the opportunity to try out the invention. After considering several alternatives, it was decided that our sister's tall walking doll would be the honoree for the first flight. Making a quick trip to the house, we retrieved it before heading to the windmill.

"Now remember what we talked about," my brother said. "This is just our first trial."

We steadily climbed up the windmill and had almost reached the top when the screaming started. Our 8-year-old sister had discovered that we had her prized possession. "Give me back my doll. You can't have her. Give her back! I'm telling mom!" Had we been on the ground, we might have paid attention, but we were high above her and intent on trying our parachute.

"Don't you dare mess up my doll! Bring her back down here!" By now her yells were frantic, and I saw her looking for rocks. We laughed because we were pretty sure she couldn't hit us.

"Ok, let's get this set," my brother instructed. There we were at the top of the world on a beautiful June day. Looking toward Crow Creek, we could see the Fleury and Mireaux homes in the distance. Looking the other way, we could almost make out the top of the Cook and Red Hail homes. We stood at the top of the platform and prepared to launch.

"Wanji, nupa, yamni, topa!" and with that we let the parachute go. For one incredible second, the doll floated, we had success, and then she plummeted to pieces on the ground below. My sister howled in distress. I scrambled down as fast as I could go.

"Wait!" my brother yelled as I headed for the hills. "We'll make some changes. Wait! Don't you remember that you're next?"

Heather Collins,
Buffalo County

Mom's Little Milking Maid

MY PARENTS STARTED MILKING COWS after they married in 1976—a time when having five kids was common and farming actually paid the bills instead of being the source of bills. Their Holstein herd remained small, usually around thirty-five to fifty head at a time. That may not seem like many, but when one has to rise at 5:30 every morning, the number can suddenly seem incredibly large.

As a youngster, my familiarity with milking was quite limited. Besides occasionally helping my sister with the feeding of calves, I had little to do with the milking operation. In fact, I spent most of my time housecleaning. I was quite content with the chore list my mother wrote for me: washing dishes, washing clothes, drying dishes, drying clothes, putting away dishes, and putting away clothes.

However, one afternoon my pleasant reverie through childhood came to a screeching halt. My mom dropped a large piece of silo unloading equipment on her foot while she was helping my dad. Though it left her with a broken foot, it did provide her with a much needed rest from the milk barn. With Mom enjoying her vacation, the milking responsibility fell on Dad's shoulders. After a few days, however, it became obvious that help was needed in the milk barn. I do not remember whose patience ran thin first—my dad's or the cows'—but I am willing to bet it was the cows'.

Since Mom's injury confined her to the house, my domestic services were no longer needed, and I was her obvious replacement in the barn. It was quite the responsibility for a fifth grader, and my dad, busy with his stock cattle and fieldwork, recruited the help of a neighbor lady to lead the milking.

After Mom's foot adequately healed, she returned to the milk barn, and I thought it only fair that I resume my household duties. However, after I had spent one hour every morning before school and two hours every evening after school for eight weeks in the milk barn, my mother thought I had potential, and with that, my role as "Mom's little milking maid" was sealed.

Mom and I were quite the team—our similar personalities helped us work well together, but sometimes our similar personalities were just a little too similar. Though I cannot recall many instances, I know Mom and I worked each other's nerves on occasion, thereby resulting in a long two-hour milking.

But it was my mother's constant presence in the barn that made the chore tolerable. In between the noise of the compressor and occasional cow bellow, my mom and I talked about everything. Our conversations did not just skim the surface but rather probed into both our minds and hearts, allowing us to connect on a deeper level emotionally and spiritually. From teachers and homework, to friends and dating; from faith and religion, to memories and dreams— she and I talked about it all.

I am older now with children of my own, but I sometimes wish I could return to the milk barn of my youth. Thanks to my mom, life was less complicated, the worries were fewer, the answers were clearer, and I knew exactly who I was—my mom's little milking maid.

Ruth Buchmann,
Rural Lesterville

Mel and Mabel

MEL AND MABEL WERE THE KIND OF NEIGHBORS everyone wishes they had. They lived according to the Golden Rule or, as the Scriptures describe the parable of the Good Samaritan, they were the good neighbor willing to help when people were in need. Times were tough in those days. The country was just coming off the Great Depression and no one had an excess of goods. There was no welfare or government surplus for needy families. Farm families were usually large because farm machinery didn't do the things they do today and there was plenty of manual labor and farm chores to do. Indian families survived by doing farm labor at peak times during the year, especially during harvest. Work was very scarce and you did the best job you could so that you might be asked to return another time for more work.

Mel was always a cheerful person, one whom I never saw upset about anything. He had a devious looking smile and gave you the impression he was about to tease you about something. You felt you had to be on guard, or he would get you.

The clearest recollection I have of Mel had to do with the geese they had at their farm. More specifically, it was the big gander that watched over the small flock as well as the place. Some people say that geese are better than watchdogs. I have no disagreement with that assumption. So when my mother sent me to their place to get some milk for my baby brother, I was hesitant because I was aware of the male goose. He would follow you around with his head low to the ground and sometimes he would let out a hiss. The adults paid little attention to him, but a little kid took him far more seriously.

About a hundred yards from their house, I had to get over a fence of woven wire with two barbed wires strung above that. It was intended to keep in sheep and small calves. It was difficult to get over the fence, and the gate was not a simple thing for a small kid to manipulate. I climbed the fence and started for their house, keeping one overly cautious eye out for the gander. I was relieved to find the gander and flock were nowhere in sight. I went to the house and gave Mabel the note from my mother. She talked to me as she filled the reused gallon lard pail I always used for drawing and hauling water from our open well. She didn't seem as threatening as I had previously thought. She placed the lid on the full pail of milk and gave it back to me. Then she handed me a cookie.

Children live in small time spans, so as I left the house, I almost completely forgot about the gander. As I walked, enjoying the fresh, still warm cookie, I was about halfway to the fence when I heard a noise beside me. I turned my head and there, not ten feet from me, was the gander! He apparently was in the creek bed that ran close to the road and around the farmstead. He came directly at me with his head down, letting out what seemed like unusually loud hisses! I was told never to show your fear or things would get worse. I walked as calmly as I could, and then a foolish thought came to me.

I could run almost as fast as my older brothers, and the fence and safety was only fifty feet away. Judging by the awkward way I had seen ducks and geese move about, I decided my chances of outrunning him were good. "Take him by surprise and get the jump on him" was my quick decision. A jackrabbit couldn't have gotten off with a better jump! Then I could hear the wings flapping and almost feel the wind, as the gander quickly closed in on me! He was right at my heels and gaining! I had no idea they could move that fast! I came to the fence and without thinking, or knowing how, I somehow cleared the fence and found myself on the other side.

Standing on safe ground, I looked back and saw the gander calmly walking back toward the house. A big flood of relief came when I realized the pail of milk was still in my hands and the lid was still intact. However, the half-eaten cookie was gone. The next thing I did was to look around to see if anyone had witnessed the event. I saw nothing and made up my mind I would keep this my little secret. Not long after that I was with my dad as he was talking with Mel, who glanced at me with that mischievous grin, "I see you like the old gander." He never said more about it. My dad never asked what he meant either. Maybe Mel thought that some things had more value when kept to oneself.

In later years, my wife and I became close friends with their son Lynn and his wife, Alpha. They, in turn, were equally good neighbors. We played a lot of cards with Lynn and Alpha before Lynn's passing, and we continue to enjoy Alpha's company and hospitality. There were times during a card game when Lynn would do a little teasing, and I would detect that same mischievous grin, and it would take me back to the voice at the creek and that speeding gander. Though I only knew him casually, Mel was kind of a special person. Maybe Mel and I shared a secret, or he might have decided to spare me any more embarrassment.

Some men have that unique ability to re-enter the world of childhood and for a brief time become a living part of it. They re-live moments of joy reserved for the simple world of the young; in so doing they enrich their own world as well. Maybe it's because at the closing years of life one finally realizes that the really important things are the simple things that are seen through the eyes of a child. A child believes all things, hopes all things, and is free of hatred. Maybe that's why God said that a person has to become like a child to enter into the kingdom of heaven. Mel and Mabel were those kinds of friends and neighbors.

Elden Lawrence,
Peever

By Greg Latza, Used with permission by Greg Latza.

A Gift for My Dad

MY DAD WAS HOSPITALIZED IN ESTELLINE for an appendectomy in 1947. At that time, this entailed about a ten-day stay. I was about nine years old. We stopped in Lake Norden on our way to visit Dad. I had five cents or ten cents so I went to the drugstore to get Dad a gift. I had seen guys punch papers out of a board and get different items. I gave my money to a clerk, pushed out a piece of paper, and they gave me a nice box of candy, which I took to the hospital for Dad. Folks must have wondered if I stole it as they questioned where I got it. They finally realized where I got it from. They then explained to me those punch boards were a form of gambling, and we should not gamble. It must have been very difficult to tell me about this, but it was done with love and it was a good lesson. I never bought a chance on a punch board again. We have also encouraged our children not to get into gambling or lottery tickets or games of chance.

Ronald Kangas,
Lake Norden

There is No Easter Bunny

THE YEAR WAS 1939, and I was five years old. I remember it as if it were yesterday.

I hung on for dear life as my brother Duane, with me behind him in the saddle, galloped our trusting horse across the prairie headed for the Lincoln One-Room School. It was located three miles from the Peters homestead, where our Dad and his Dad before him, then both Duane and I, were born in a small two-story house.

A big rabbit hopped out of the brush near us and scampered away.

I yelled, "Oh, I bet that is the Easter Bunny!"

I almost lost my hold on the back of the saddle as I turned to watch. I just couldn't miss out on this exciting frenzy!

Duane's harsh reply I have never forgotten. He shouted, "There is no Easter Bunny!"

To this day I have never forgiven him for this. When Mom was trying to soothe me after we arrived home that day and we were savoring her delicious home made bread, Duane seemed certain he had done the right thing.

"Anyone who is old enough to go to school needs to know there is NO Easter bunny!" he firmly announced.

Jeanne Kirsch,
Rural White Lake

The Rowan School in Sanborn County

THE ROWAN SCHOOL, six and one-half miles north of Artesian, played the role of teaching, political, and entertainment site. Having come from Wisconsin, where schools had already been established, my Grandfather Pat Rowan realized that his community had to support an educational program. With thirteen children of his own, in 1893 he became the first chairman of Benedict I. The minutes tell us that "they decided they needed $250 for the year; the Teacher would receive $125, Coal $30, Painting $30, Plastering $10, and Incidentals $40. It was decided to have six months of school. The four-month term for winter to commence about the first of November. The two-month spring term to commence about the first of April. Have male teacher for the winter term. For spring term the Board should do the best they could."

The February 23, 1895, minutes of the Benedict I school district read, "Motion made and carried that the schoolhouse be sealed inside above the wainscoting, to be of good material and the work to be done in workmanlike manner. Also, to be painted with two coats of light blue paint. The ceiling is to be of smooth ceiling three feet above the wainscoting on both sides and the east end to be used for blackboards, to be painted black with such material as is used for such purpose. All labor and material to be furnished by the contractor and the work to be done during the month of March 1895. All bids to be in the Clerk's office by the 10th of March, 1895. The Board to have the right to accept or reject any and all bids."

Thus, Benedict I school became the hub of our community. Each Christmas, children, parents, grandparents, and neighbors drove their wagons, buggies, and later autos, to watch the magic of the candles on the towering pine tree light up expectant faces. Hushed silence ensued. Of course, the white candles had to be extinguished very soon to keep the tree from catching on fire. Then, sleigh bells announced the arrival of Santa shouting, "Ho! Ho! Ho! Merry Christmas, everyone!"

In the center of the building, a huge pot-bellied stove not only heated our classroom, but also provided the most delicious lunches. Each pupil brought a potato to school. At recess time we stuck our potatoes in the cinders under the pot belly. At noon, without any butter or even salt and pepper, we enjoyed the most mouth-watering gourmet potatoes.

The school house became a public forum during election time. Candidates proclaimed their virtues to large crowds, who were vitally interested in the workings of their government. After the formal discussion, hot coffee, pie, and cake turned the meeting into a party.

Box or basket socials earned money for certain projects. All women, single or married, prepared a lunch for two and packed it in a decorated basket or box. One of the men would raffle these off to the highest bidder. If a fellow had a certain girl with whom he wished to eat, he would have to pay a high price, because the other men would have fun "bidding up" the desired box. Not only did the school raise money, but everyone had a good time.

By the middle of the century, the one-room school houses became fewer and fewer. However, the one-room school house teachers brought more than learning to their students; they taught the values of a fulfilled life.

Eleanore Rowan Moe,
Sanborn County

Baking Mud Pies

THE PLAYHOUSE WAS AN OPEN-AIR KITCHEN on the edge of the slough, under towering cottonwoods on our family farm by Lake Norden. This was an opportunity to bake, cook, and invent the mud pies and other masterpieces to keep us busy during the summers of our youth. It was also close to the house for mom to keep an eye on us. Hours were spent with our cousins and other friends who came to play, cooking the wonders of mud.

All the supplies were readily available: our door-less refrigerator, old wood-burning stove, table and chairs, all kinds of plates, silverware, pots and pans, and coffee pots. Easily available were leaves for mud pies, water from the slough or horse trough, all kinds of dirt to dig, sticks, and, of course, when making coffee, the "coffee weed." I still don't know what it was, but when the small seeds at the top turned brown, it was the coffee. We also had cinnamon—a brick scraped with holes in it to loosen the brick dust. The fuzz from cattails from the slough also came in handy.

One summer day, Joyce, my sister, two years older, and I were busy baking mud pies. On that day we didn't have enough ingredients. Having watched mom and our three older sisters bake, we knew that we needed eggs. Off to the hen house we ran to collect our eggs for our wonderful mud pies to be prepared that day. We were busy cracking, mixing, and baking when a certain mother of ours, Margaret Kangas, appeared. Needless to say, that was the last time we used eggs in our mud pie. Her attitude toward our using the needed ingredients and using the eggs she sold for extra money at the egg house in Lake Norden was less than happy. The lecture and spanking that resulted deterred us from ever trying that again. Plus, the next day the stench of those pies was incredibly bad. Being caught wasn't enough. We had to dispose of those smelly pies in a place far away from the playhouse, down in the slough.

Sonja Stormo,
Rural Lake Norden

Hunting and Trapping

HUNTING AND TRAPPING WERE A BIG PART OF MY LIFE growing up on the farm in Faulk County, and it also provided some income for me. There were always lots of rabbits to hunt, with a bounty on them of two cents to five cents. Eventually, it got up to twenty-five cents. I went rabbit hunting by the creeks, and then, later in the day, I would go home and get the wagon to pick up all the rabbits I had shot. After I got them back home, I hung them on the north side of the old school house, which was situated in the middle of the farmyard. Every so often, I took the rabbits to Chelsea to get money for them. I also trapped skunks and muskrats. I often would smoke the skunks out of culverts or holes they were in, and if they didn't come out, I'd take a barbwire and fish down in to pull them out. This usually was the safest way to avoid getting sprayed, but not always. With skunks, the width of stripe determined how much they were worth. I would skin the skunks and melt down the skunk fat. This oil or grease made excellent shoe or leather grease. And, no, the oil didn't stink! The pelts were worth $1.50 to $2.00 apiece.

It seemed for many years the countryside was overrun with rabbits, and there was always an abundance of pheasants. With so many rabbits around, there were a lot of rabbit hunts. Everyone would get together with their pickups and trucks. The vehicles would line up around a quarter of land, and then the men hunted until they met in the middle. When the hunting was over, everyone would finish up at the Chelsea Hall for oyster stew. There were also pheasant drives held in the area. Again, everyone gathered together to hunt four quarters of land at once. After the hunt, which usually yielded lots of pheasants, all the birds would be taken to Aberdeen to the canteen for the soldiers.

Adelbert Rawden,
Chelsea
Submitted by Karla Rawden Pritchard

FAMILY

SD State Agricultural Heritage Museum Photographic Collection.

Family Time

ON THE FAMILY FARM NEAR AURORA, winter evenings during the 1930s were long and quiet; I remember them as warm, comfortable, family times. All of us gathered around the round oak kitchen table to read and play games with Mom and Pop. Our light source in the kitchen was kerosene lamps and later an Aladdin lamp, a mantle lamp that provided more adequate light. We were all avid readers, relying on our teacher to borrow books for us from the library in Flandreau; we owned few books ourselves. Zane Grey and Horatio Alger were among our favorite authors. Our parents subscribed to the "Sioux Falls Argus Leader," which was delivered a day late with the mail. It was our only source of news, since we had no radio. Even after we got one in 1936, we seldom listened to it in the evening.

As children, I and my brothers learned to play many card games. We also became quite skilled at caroms, a form of laptop billiards. A square board with pockets in the four corners is placed on a table or on the knees of two to four players. The object of the game was to snap the caroms, which were similar to checkers, into the pockets using one's fingers. As a result of our years playing caroms, Les made the billiards team at college and was quite a pool shark. Mom, who considered "pool" a dirty word, was stunned to learn of Les's prowess at billiards.

At bedtime, nine p.m., we three brothers would head to the upstairs room, which was furnished with a portable closet and a bed at each end. We slept together in a double-sized bed at the east end of the room, with me crowded into the middle. Hired men or visiting cousins used the other bed. The upstairs was drafty and cold in the winter. Answering a call of nature in the middle of the night, especially in winter, was a task to be avoided, if possible. At one point, it occurred to Les that we could simply pee out the window. When

Mom one day noticed a yellow stain running down the siding from the upstairs window, the practice came to an abrupt end.

Norman D. Thomsen,
Rural Brookings

Blizzard Bliss

LIVING ON A CATTLE RANCH in south-central South Dakota provided me with many opportunities as well as hardships. Reflecting upon my childhood, I am reminded of how blessed I truly am. From the good times, where rain showed itself as plentiful and the grass thrived, to the hard times, when drought, sickness, or loss seemed unbearable, growing up on a South Dakota ranch was full of moments designed for character building.

One of these memorable moments occurred in the winter of 1997. Our calving season had just begun, and, like any late February in South Dakota, it was cold. The weather stations predicted a major winter storm, and my family was working to prepare for it. The heifers that were due to calve were in the close pens, and the barn was ready with many stalls filled knee-deep with straw as we waited for the blizzard to arrive. Then it finally hit. Clouds rolled in and the snow blew with extreme intensity. The wind and snow came with such force it felt as though ice crystals were cutting into any exposed skin it could find.

Just as we suspected, the blizzard spurred on the increase of heifers calving. I was just seven years old, and I can still remember going out to help get the heifers in and checking on newborn calves. That was how our family worked; all of us needed and wanted to help in times of hardship. Suddenly, all electricity went out and the snow began to pile up. Living on a ranch demanded that we be prepared for this sort of event. Dad hooked up the 15,000-watt generator to the house so that we could stay warm. After we finished supper, the generator was dragged to the barn, where the baby calves were trying desperately to keep warm.

I often refer to this event as one of my fondest memories. Even with the demanding labor, the biting cold, and physical exhaustion, working with my family made this a wonderful experience for me. Living in rural South Dakota has instilled in me the importance of family. We leaned on each other in difficult times. With no source of power in the house, candle light brightened our home and family became the only means of entertainment. Long into the night we played cards, mostly Pitch, Whist, and Go Fish. In between games, Dad took breaks to check on the restless heifers, waiting for the perfect time for the miracle of birth. This was how we spent our time during the "Blizzard of '97."

I had many lessons of responsibility, respect, hard work, and perseverance that were an ever present part of life growing up on a ranch. But it was the love, teamwork, guidance, and care of the family that was the best part of my childhood. The ranch was not just a place to live or grow up; it was a home—my home. Growing up within my rural, South Dakota family, I understood that the hard times we experienced were never bad times. Rather, they were my major source of happiness.

Wyatt DeJong,
Kennebec

Kenneth and Hilda: The Beginning

ONLY FIVE WEEKS AFTER MEETING HILDA, Kenneth proposed at the dance hall in Harrold where they'd had their first dance, proving he wasn't just stubborn, but efficient as well. He'd carried with him an idea of the perfect girl since he was a boy. It was loosely based on everything his mother wasn't: warm, kind, loving, compassionate, and feminine. It's not that he didn't love his mother, because he honestly did, and every time his thoughts strayed to her, gone now five years, he felt the emptiness. But his mother was a different breed of woman, a first-generation American born to Norwegian immigrants. She was built for the prairie, with broad shoulders and stocky legs. Her clothes, like her body, were crafted for practicality and function, not beauty. Her dresses hung like potato sacks, roomy enough for when she was squatting with the milk cows and light enough to withstand the afternoon sun when she was working the fields. Her hands, the few times she reached for Kenneth to pat him on the back or to quickly hug his shoulders, were calloused and rough. Her voice, too. And while Kenneth knew his mother had loved him fiercely, he could not remember her ever telling him so.

Kenneth had watched his parents struggle with the land, had watched them brush past each other in the house, rarely glancing at one another. They were business partners first and foremost; marriage was an afterthought. Kenneth wanted something different, something more. He wanted a wife with smooth skin and a honey voice. He wanted to be successful enough that she would never have to dirty her hands in order to help provide. He wanted to give her a home, beautiful clothes, her own car. He wanted a wife who reached for him the minute he walked through the door. He wanted love.

He saw all of this when he saw Hilda. So he went down on one knee like a gentleman for her so she'd know he meant business. He had it planned out perfectly. He paid a guy to start the song at exactly 9:15 p.m., enough time for them to dance to a handful of songs after she said yes, after their future of husband and wife was a reality. He'd bought a new suit for the occasion, not wanting to ask the question in something faded. He'd gotten a haircut and a shave and told the boys at the barber's the whole plan. He'd washed, waxed, and swept the car out. And, as the icing on the cake, surprised her with a half dozen red roses and a box of chocolate covered cherries, two of her favorite things—information that he'd managed to coax out of her sister Ida.

As soon as the first few notes of Dorsey's song found its way to them, Kenneth kneeled. He looked up at her earnestly, his pin-striped tie askew beneath his sweater vest, brown socks peeking out beneath black slacks (he'd not had enough money to buy matching socks), and the room quieted as the dancers parted around them, eager to see what was happening. His proposal was straightforward and to the point: he loved her, she was beautiful, and he couldn't spend another night without her.

Hilda laughed, refused, and laughed again. "Kenneth, you goof. Are you punch-drunk, or do you always go around proposing to girls after only a few dates?" Kenneth's smile died away and he got slowly to his feet. She stared at him, but he just kept dusting his knees off with his hands. She covered her mouth in surprise when she realized he was serious.

"Oh," she said softly. "I'm sorry, I didn't think—."

"We oughta go, don't you think? Get you home before your pop wonders what happened to you."

Hilda grabbed for his arm, but he stepped away, grabbing her coat and holding it open for her. They walked out the door miles apart. In the car, Kenneth turned the radio up too loudly for either of them to talk.

Courtney Huse Wika,
Pierre

Resting on the Oven Door

MARIA WAS A MID-WIFE helping neighbors and many in the community of Sinai when new babies arrived and when illness struck. She would leave her family for days and go and care for the expectant mother and the family until the mother was able to take care of her baby and her family again. Many times she and Dr. Scanlan and Dr. Torvick would leave in the wagon and sled not knowing if they could make it or not because of weather and roads. Marie would tell of many times when the doctors could not make it, and Mons, Maria's husband, would have to take her, leaving their young family at home. Maria would also talk about arriving at a home where there was no heat, nothing to burn and little to eat; it was then that Mons would have to stay and help too. The new baby that arrived would then have to be kept on the oven door to survive. Maria baptized many babies that she thought would not live.

Phyllis Bolstad Hanson,
Sinai

Deep in the Heart of Texas: No Bang to That One

THE EARLY FIFTIES FOUND US DOING WELL on our little farm. My husband John worked two days a week at the local livestock sale barns, in addition to doing his Dad's farming. He was a busy man. The older kids and I did chores and some of the fieldwork to help out. Our family was happy playing together and riding horses. The youngest of our four children, Roger, was five years old in 1956 when another baby girl arrived.

I will remember the day we brought Peggy Lee, named by her father, home from the hospital. Four anxious siblings were leaning over the car front seat remarking, "Isn't she cute." Little did I realize that in just eighteen months she'd be on a horse, riding with the rest of them. She was not a little girl for long as she was always outside with older kids, riding or grooming the horses. We had several little Shetland ponies. She was always our brave one.

When she was seven, she wanted to dress in cowboy clothes and enter a local talent show. A plan was devised. She would sing "Deep in the Heart of Texas" and shoot off her twin cap guns at the appropriate times. Her Dad, older brothers, and a brother-in-law served as her band. Her guns were loaded and she was ready. But when the time came to shoot her guns, the caps burnt off and would not feed through. She looked at her Dad, wondering what to do. He nodded his head and she went on to sing the rest of her song minus the bangs. She was always willing to try anything, and to finish what she started.

This year when I broke my hip, she drove me nearly 200 miles to the Sanford Hospital in Sioux Falls. We pulled into the emergency entrance at Sanford Hospital just three hours after the break. She has always been a brave one.

Della Studt,
Rural Presho

Winter Saturdays

WITH SEVEN CHILDREN TO RAISE AND FEED on a farm near Bryant, Dad always had chores for us to do. No different than any other day, Saturday would start out with milking the cows. It may have been about fifteen cows, but it seemed like it was thirty or more. After getting the milking done and the livestock fed and watered, we would all head to the house for a big breakfast

Soon after our breakfast came the real Saturday chore—cleaning the barn. Getting the tractor with the manure spreader as close to the barn door as possible, five boys with pitchforks in hand went to work. A couple of hours and several loads later the barn was ready for another week, with clean, fresh bedding.

After an afternoon of fun and games with the family (sometimes neighbors, too) and the evening milking, we were ready for the sauna and a good night's sleep.

If we only knew then how good we really had it.

Winfred Noem,
Rural Bryant

My Father's Kingdom

OUR FARM WAS MY FATHER'S KINGDOM. There were no pearly gates or golden streets. A wire gate and a dusty road led to the farmstead rimmed by the Jim River and Timber Creek. There were fields of beauty in rough pasture, fertile land, and black furrows. My dad would love to say, "Mother and I are not limited by a boss who tells us what we can and can't do. What we plan and how many hours we work are our limitation—that and the weather. We are blessed to live in God's creation, with the sky above, the earth below, sunrise and sunset, all of nature, the weather, and birds and animals." Dad never acted like a monarch, although he frequently referred to his "kingdom," in which my mother was his full partner in planning and work.

With love and direction, we six children became part of the workforce of the farm. Dad or Mom would say, "We are proud that you are old enough and strong enough to help the family with chores. Do them right away and do them well." We learned to work at assigned chores. Stalls were cleaned, hay was hauled, cows were milked, and cobs were recycled from the hog yard for cook stove fuel. At the close of the day, all the subjects of our kingdom gathered around the supper table, centered by a kerosene lamp. Bowls of steaming food were on the oilcloth awaiting us. There was laughter and conversation. Everyone had something to say.

My father's kingdom was only one of many in the thirties and forties. South Dakota was filled with productive farms. Now you can still find South Dakota family farms operated by good people. Our nation and the whole world are filled with confident, hard working, can-do people who say, "I was raised on a South Dakota Farm."

Marian Cramer,
Frankfort

Banking in My Dad's Blue Bib Overalls

MY PARENTS LOST EVERY PENNY THEY HAD in savings and their checking account. They had written a check in the amount of $700 just a few days before the bank closed, but it had not cleared the bank. From then on my dad always carried our family savings in the upper pocket of his blue bib overalls. He pinned the pocket closed with a large safety pin. His friends kidded him about his bank as many of them kept their savings in the same manner. For many years after the banks closed, no one trusted depositing the little money they had in a bank.

> *Dorothy Edwards Weinberger,*
> *Artesian*

Dad

AS A CHILD GROWING UP ON THE FARM, every day was an exciting adventure. When I was very young, my Dad did most of his fieldwork with a team of horses. Early in the morning just as the sun was making its appearance in the eastern sky, Dad would be hitching up a team of gentle horses to a piece of machinery. There would be a break at noon for the horses to rest, drink some cool well water, and eat some hay. Not only did the horses need a break from the hot sun, so did Dad. Mom would set a hot meal on the table and the radio would be turned to WNAX for the news and the all-important grain and livestock reports. Then it was back to the field and the hot sun.

As the heat of the day was fading, and the sun began to lower itself in the western sky, I would watch for the big brown horses and my Dad as they turned into the lane. I knew the workday was over. My legs could not carry me fast enough to meet him. He stopped the horses, bent down, and lovingly lifted me on the back of the big sweaty horse we named Nell. For a little while, I was a Queen, riding the rest of the way home, my blond hair blowing in the late afternoon breeze, looking over my small world. No one needed to tell the horses that the next stop would be the water tank. I would hang on to the harness so I would not slip down their neck for an unwanted bath. Back in the barn, the horses were fed and slept for the night. When the feeding was done and the harness was put away, Dad would lift me down.

I would say, "I'll meet you again tomorrow, Daddy."

Millie Petersen,
Centerville

Homework

DAD WAS ONE OF THE ONLY MEN who promoted and built Logan Consolidated School. Logan was one of the first consolidated schools in the state with twelve grades. All of us kids graduated from high school there except Donald, who finished at Raymond school. Then we all attended and graduated from SDSU. On winter evenings, we did our homework in the kitchen. Sometimes we sat at the kitchen table. If we were reading, we would sit in chairs around the cook stove as the fire was dying down. We opened the oven door, took off our shoes, and warmed our feet on the open oven door. We often had apples, popcorn (which we grew), and cocoa for snacks. My brother always wanted "Sis" to make the cocoa. I think that's because I used more cocoa powder and made it sweeter than Mom did!

Melba Olverson,
Raymond

Our New Car

IT WAS 1926, when Dad's buggy, which he'd driven for so many years, was getting old and starting to go to pieces. Dad then used the farm wagon and drove the team seven and one-half miles to our little town for the groceries, coal, lumber, or whatever. Mom was starting to hate the wagon. It was so slow and obnoxious, and other people already had cars.

Dad started thinking and talking about getting a car. It was a big decision and money was not plentiful. Finally the day came. Dad walked to a neighbor's house and rode with them to town. Mom, my sister, brother, and I stayed at home. We were so excited. We kept ourselves busy to overcome the tension. We scrubbed, cleaned, and polished—everything must be clean and in place. We were getting a new car!

Dad stayed in town all day to be shown how to drive and care for the car. About four o'clock, Dad slowly came around the curve and down the road to our house—in a new car! Everyone waited for him to stop. Then we ran out the door, excited beyond words. It was here at last, our new car! We looked it over good! We made many trips from the house to the car before dark. It was a shiny black 1926 Model T Ford—a two-seated touring car bought from Kirpatrick's Ford Shop in Faith. It had a lot of new extras—demountable rims, electric starter and lights, and a water pump. A hand crank was used if the starter didn't function. It had removable window curtains and panes of thick, clear plastic for windows. These "curtains" clamped onto the tops of the doors and were taken off for the warm months. The heavy patent leather "top" could be unclamped from the windshield and folded back into a roll like a convertible. Little Irean tried desperately to talk Dad into doing that. How she would have liked to have had the sun and wind in her face and hair! Dad never complied. He got enough sun and wind out in the fields and doing chores, and besides, he was not taking a chance on ruining the car top by putting creases in it.

Two levers, one on each side of the steering column, were the gas and the "spark." On the floor were three peddles—the brake, reverse, and low. The seats were covered with shiny, black patent leather. The car cost $625.00.

Dad soon had a lean-to built onto our granary. The Model T was kept in the garage when it was not being used. Before going anywhere Dad always checked the oil, gas, water, tires, and battery. We always left with plenty of time to get there. Dad drove between twenty-five and thirty-five miles an hour. It carried our eggs and cream to town and our groceries and hardware home.

The Model T lasted fifteen years, still working and looking the same as the day Dad bought it, but it was way out of style. He sold it to a neighbor boy for $25 and bought a new red Ford pickup!

What I wouldn't give to have that ol' Model T Ford!

Irean Jordan,
Perkins County

COMMUNITY

SD State Agricultural Heritage Museum Photographic Collection.

Saturday Nights in the Twenties and Thirties

THE ARTESIAN TOWN BAND town band blared out Sousa's "Stars and Stripes Forever." The farmers and townspeople mingled in front of the wooden bandstand to applaud the efforts of their loved ones and neighbors. Automobiles lined both sides of Main Street. Older folks sat in the autos closer to the bandstand. Sometimes the townspeople parked in front of the bandstand between six and seven o'clock so they could get a closer parking spot. The band was a cross-section of the population, ranging anywhere from seventh grade students to senior citizens. Practice on Wednesday evenings preceded the Saturday night concerts.

On Saturday evenings, the farmers quit work early, indulged in a bath, and were on Main Street by 7:00 or 7:30. All the farmers from miles around brought in their egg crates and cream cans. The women would place their grocery orders before the start of the concert, listen to the concert, and then chat with their friends and neighbors on the streets and in the stores or with those sitting in autos. The men shopped for hardware supplies, new overalls, work shirts, socks, and tobacco.

The main food attraction was the popcorn machine. Popcorn, with its tantalizing aroma, cost just five cents. When I had eaten half the bag of popcorn, I returned to ask the owner for more butter. He never refused. Later I learned that the popcorn wagon was a front for moonshine whiskey sales. Prohibition was in force at the time.

The second most popular spot was Foote's Drug Store, with its marble counter, turn-around stools, and huge mirror on the wall. Cokes were sold only at the soda fountain. Those soda fountain drinks and mouth-watering ice cream floats were well worth the dime. Also, Johnson's Hotel had ice cream chairs and small marble tables, where I could order ice cream in an aluminum dish with a paper liner. Two scoops cost a dime. Then I could top it off with a five-cent bag of

Planter's peanuts.

The smoke-filled pool hall was a mecca for pool players and the men who exchanged farm planting or harvesting tips, better ways to raise cows and hogs, the best fence posts to buy, the best mash for the hogs, and which vet or farmer could do the best castrating.

In Artesian, movie fans could attend on Wednesday, Saturday, and Sunday evenings. Anyone who bought a Saturday ticket could go free on Sunday. In the late twenties, these were silent movies, but a talented musician played the piano to fit the actions on the screen as the audience read the script across the bottom of the screen. My first silent movie was Harriet Beecher Stowe's "Uncle Tom's Cabin."

On Saturday nights, the Artesian population doubled; the Artesian "family" reveled in its weekly reunion.

Eleanore Rowan Moe,
Artesian

Social Life in the Thirties

ALTHOUGH FARMS WERE HALF A MILE OR SO from one another and transportation was sometimes a challenge, we rarely felt lonely or isolated. The farms in our neighborhood of Brookings County formed a tightly knit community that came together in bad times as well as good.

A neighborhood constituted those living within approximately a one- to two-mile radius. Most of our neighbors—the Greves, Krogmans, Ericksons, Styfs, Steuks, Lunschens, Rangs, and Duffs—were German or Dutch. We were the only Danish family. The Greves, a childless couple who were exceptionally good to us children, were especially close friends. We all got along and knew we could depend on one another, not only for social life, but also for help and survival. Neighbor helped neighbor whenever help was needed. Some of our neighbors had cars, while others, like us, had only trucks. Those who had cars offered rides when necessary, and those with trucks helped with hauling when needed. There was never any hesitation to ask for help and never any expectation of being compensated.

There were no phones in the immediate neighborhood, so local news traveled on foot or through neighborhood gatherings. The phone closest to us was at the Bulens' farm, a mile away, directly across our section of land. The approach of the Bulens to our farm usually foretold of an emergency, an illness, or a death—the likely reasons for phone messages in those days.

Despite the hours of labor, people found time for neighborhood get-togethers. Even in winter, when roads were impassable, friends and neighbors gathered—traveling by bobsled for evenings of 500 Rummy. The card games usually ended by eleven p.m. when the travelers would hitch up their horses and ride home on bobsleds.

The need to share equipment and labor turned many tasks into social events. Threshing required the cooperation of the entire neighborhood. Corn shelling usually involved two or three neighbors working together; one neighbor loaned the sheller, and others helped with the work. No one had upright silos, but many farmers in those days had trench silos, made by digging a trench eight to ten feet deep and perhaps fifty yards long. Filling the silo required a cutter owned by one of the neighbors. With the help of three or four bundle carriers, the average silo could be filled in a couple of days. Clearing the snow and repairing wind-damaged buildings were also neighborhood projects. Although the work was hard, it was natural to work together, and the resulting camaraderie turned these projects into pleasurable gatherings.

Norman D. Thomsen,
Rural Brookings

From Bombay to Butte County

THE 1960s WERE A TIME OF CHANGE in America: the Civil Rights movement, the women's movement, the arrival of the Beatles, the advent of the counterculture when hair grew longer and beards became common, and when man set foot on the moon. In 1968 I set foot in South Dakota. I may as well have landed on the moon.

In 1967 I was a Bombay socialite just returned home from a year in London and travel in Europe. I was at loose ends and a friend suggested I take a job at the Peace Corps office. I met my husband, Jerry, who was stationed in Bombay as a Peace Corps volunteer. Less than a year later we were married and on our way to America.

Arrival at the Jacobsen sheep ranch in Butte County was in the night—the darkest night I had ever experienced. At daylight, I went outside to look around. I had come from Bombay, (pop., ten million) to Castle Rock (pop., seven). Many years later I found words that described how I felt: "The world opened wider than I had ever known it and instantly a delicious tension came over me . . . It seemed to settle on me from the giant sky and I knew from the beginning that it had something to do with distance, the endless grass, and the sweep of eternal wind . . . . I understood then that I was in a different world, and that I was now blessed with access to the entire sky." (*The Contract Surgeon* by Dan O'Brien).

The Jacobsen family expressed much warmth and excitement around my presence. I felt at home and very welcome. There was much to learn. This was not the Hollywood America I had anticipated. We used an outhouse because water was delivered in a truck and had to be conserved. The Wendt boys and the Carlson boys were elderly brothers from neighboring ranches. The Jolly Juniors Extension Club members were women over fifty who had started meeting in their youth. The radio broadcast, constant in the kitchen, was punctuated with ads from the "Jolly Funeral Home" (I later learned that "Jolley" was a family name).

Lambing season was in, and there was a lot of activity connected with that. I helped in the shed with branding and docking lambs, feeding bum lambs with a soda pop bottle, and in the house with cooking, laundry, everything. Having grown up with servants, my work experience was limited.

There were many opportunities for miscommunication between my heavy British accent and the fast-talking, jargon-filled American language. For instance, a few days after I arrived, my brother-in-law Chuck said, "I'm going to town to get parts. Want to ride along?" As we sped along the deserted highway in the pickup, I marveled at all the space, the endless horizon. We went to Belle Fourche, the first of many rides to town, which could also mean Newell, Sturgis, or Spearfish. I noticed the cars. So many colors—bright red, royal blue, gold, orange, yellow, kelly green, and turquoise. On the way back to the ranch, I commented to Chuck, "You don't see many black caahs around here." He pondered on it and replied, "This is Hereford country."

Fee Jacobsen,
Butte County

Living in Two Worlds

SUPPOSE YOU WERE ABLE TO SOMEHOW OBTAIN a totally different perspective on human life. In other words, be able to see the world in another cultural perspective. That's what the Indian people had to do; not by choice, but through a necessity imposed on them. In a clash of two different cultures, a hunting and gathering way of life was upended, new ways were imposed, and indigenous people had no choice but to adopt new ways of doing things and new ways of seeing a different world.

The Dakota Indians observed the moon cycles and kept a mental clock of the times and seasons. Living in close harmony with nature, they were able to determine to an exact day when to harvest wild plants and berries. Superb hunting skills were enhanced by an instinctive, intuitive knowledge. They were also able to know when weather changes were to occur and whether it would be a daily change or a seasonal shift. This ability was the result of the intuitive knowledge they obtained from being close observers of the natural world and its laws. French Jesuits were amazed at the knowledge the American Indians had of the natural sciences. They wrote in their reports about how even the little children were more advanced in the knowledge of the natural sciences than were their learned scholars in France.

In the early 1950s, I was on the cutting edge of changes in our old way of life and those brought on by living and working with a young, thriving farm community. The result of this partial assimilation was living in two worlds that were often directly opposed to each other. The basic difference in the cultures is that the mainstream American sees himself as an individual while the Indian regards himself as a part of the whole of creation. The Creator is at the center of the Indian's world, while the individualist sees himself at the center of his world. The Indian believes every living thing has rights and that natural laws are the highest form of law and should take precedence over man-made laws. Because of the dominance of written laws, Indians became a survivalist culture.

Meeting basic survival needs kept life simple. However, I believe, like many of my elders, that our people are at their best when surviving. In a survivalist culture, a common struggle seems to bring the people closer together and make them more sensitive toward the needs of each other. By contrast, the competitive, selfish lifestyle brings out the worst in us and encourages selfishness and hoarding. It is when we are surviving that our senses and intuitive knowledge are also at their peak and when we share oneness with all creation.

With each passing elder, more of the old ways vanish as the old wise ones take what they have with them on their journey to the spirit world. The young ones don't need someone who watches the sunset to tell them what the weather will be like; they can go inside and turn on the television and watch the weather channel.

Elden Lawrence,
Peever

Picking Rock

WE GREW UP ON THE EDGE of wheat and corn fields. We watched our neighbors through the years come in the spring time with their tractors, plows, and disks to prepare the acres of black soil near our home for spring planting, and then they would return later to seed the fertile fields. When the long summer days came, those seeds pushed up out of the land to change into amber shafts of wheat and tall stalks of green corn. Under the hot July winds that blew out of the western sky, those bountiful fields glistened and shimmered in the distance like mirages. While our family was not farmers like our neighbors, the Kuschel brothers or the Oletzke family, we understood farm families and their strong bonds to their way of life. Through their presence in our young lives, my brothers and I learned the art of hard work, self-reliance, and taking care of ourselves. In time, these values would take us far in our lives.

In many ways we were different from our neighbors; not quite like night and day, but close to it. We are Dakota Indians. We had strong attachments to land and place, too. We still spoke our language at home. Our family relationships were extensive and connected like a large spider web. Our home was a small, four-room house on a high hill overlooking Lake Traverse on the South Dakota side. Our father built that house himself in 1936 with the help of his brothers-in-law, Samson and Herbert. From this vantage point, we saw the internal distance in our lives that separated us from our neighbors, but the expanse of the South Dakota prairie afforded us a chance to dream and imagine possibilities of the larger world. We sank our memory into the land like someone investing money in a lifelong venture to always remember. We knew our land and its natural contours intimately in the way people know the backs of their hands. But the strongest bond that kept us together was the idea of family. We lived in a place and time that blended elements of two different cultures together into a distinctive way of interpreting the world about us. We had our feet planted in two cultures, taking the best qualities from each. Thus, at an early age, from our farmer neighbors, my brothers and I learned the value of hard work as a way to make our way in the world. So when we saw a neighbor drive into our yard early in the morning, we knew he wanted to hire us to pick rock in one of his fields.

In retrospect, picking rock seemed like drudgery even for young Indian boys, but we gladly went with one of the neighbors to work for a day or two, walking through acres of planted crops and picking rocks. But we were young, strong, and full of vigor. After the wagon was filled with rocks of various sizes, we took it to the edge of the field and dumped the rocks into deep ravines. Our hard work would then start all over. As we walked and picked rock, we enjoyed the easy humor of our neighbors, who regaled us with hilarious stories. From far out in the fields we sometimes observed towering white thunderheads in the vast South Dakota sky, expanding with a promise of rain and wind. While we were separated by a cultural divide, we were still able to catch glimpses of each other's way of life that seemed to make us ponder what we heard and saw, however brief. When noon time came, we broke for dinner, and what hearty and splendid meals awaited us at their farm houses! After all of that walking up and down through long fields and the heavy lifting of rocks that refused to budge so easily, we needed to restore ourselves.

One of the best parts of picking rock was the huge meals waiting for us: large bowls of mashed potatoes, brown gravy, steamed vegetables, large platters of baked pork chops, and all the ice cream we could eat. We savored this food, because it was different from what we ate at home. But the sum of all these youthful experiences would take many years for us to fully appreciate and understand. Through our experiences with the hard work of picking rock for our neighbors we gained insight into the ideas of hard work and self-reliance that would become cornerstones in our lives. In time, my brothers and I went away to the armed services and off to college. One of us never came home; two of us enlisted in the Navy and saw much of the world. I went off to college in California and eventually returned home, transformed by new ideas about life. Through all of these changes, we never forgot the values passed on to us by our neighbors.

Harvey DuMarce,
Lake Traverse area

The Cookie Jar

IT IS SEPTEMBER 25, 2006. This morning was another trip to the Vienna Post Office for a.m. coffee. Myra Cluts has a large square table in the Post Office lobby. She makes coffee for the local coffee drinkers. There are bakery goods on the table, including her good homemade donuts. There is no menu here. No prices. Just leave a donation in the cookie jar on the table. This is a unique relaxing coffee shop. You don't hear shouting and rarely a curse. No dice cups to bang the table. I get to Vienna about once a week to listen in and enjoy. After coffee, I like to spend the rest of the morning and noon hour with our daughter, Carol Reddig, and her family.

Ronald Kangas,
Vienna

The Church's Role in Farm Life

"GLOOM AND DOOM" does not describe life on the farm in the twenties and thirties. We did not possess the high tech machines and labor-saving devices of today, but we were happy folks. The church played a vital role in the community. Glenview Congregational Church, four miles north of Fedora, was a focal point for entertainment. My mother, Bessie Smith Rowan, was the teacher for the young folks, who numbered twenty to thirty. On Sunday mornings, the stage was full. In the center, the minister stood behind the pulpit. On one side sat the orchestra of ten to fifteen enthusiastic novices; on the other, the old piano and the choir.

Along with worship, these young folks anticipated the home parties where everyone participated in "Spin the Bottle," "Charades," "Gossip," and card games with hot chocolate served in the winter and Kool-Aid or ice water in the summer. We played volleyball or baseball in the summer. Often the parents accompanied their children so they "could get caught up" on the latest community news. At Christmas time, we exchanged home-made gifts: perhaps an embroidered tea towel, a hot pad, or a crude carving. The most creative party was Halloween, when we made our costumes from the rag bags and our imagination.

Winter Sunday afternoons, the young folks gathered at a frozen creek or pond for ice skating. Everyone helped everyone else get their skates on. Afterwards, somebody's mother would treat us to hot chocolate and goodies.

Summer ice-cream socials and the fall turkey suppers brought revenue for the pastor's salary. Everyone with an ice cream freezer gathered at the church a few hours early to smash the ice (cut on the Jim River and stored at the Artesian Ice Company) into fine crystals; then each would take turns turning the crank of the freezer until the egg, sugar, and cream mixture became heavy. One precaution throughout the procedure was using salt to melt the ice but never letting it get into the ice cream. Next, the ice cream was packed carefully with more salt, the water was let out of the little hole towards the bottom of the freezer, and a blanket or tarp was placed over the wooden freezer until serving time. Sometimes the ladle was removed, to the delight of anyone in the area, as this "tasting time" ladle was covered with the most delicious ice cream.

The fall turkey suppers took months to plan as this meant ten to fifteen turkeys, pounds of potatoes, dozens of pumpkin and apple pies, home made biscuits, and gallons of coffee. None of this was prepared in the modern kitchen of today. Women baked the turkeys at home in their coal, wood, or cow-chip fed ovens. The potatoes were cooked on gas burners, which some farmers brought for the occasion. Then the men would mash these potatoes in huge pots. They were kept hot by placing the potato pots in dishpans of hot water. Most of the other foods were transported on the big day to the church. Everybody in the congregation had a job as folks would come from twenty to fifty miles for the evening of food, conversation, and seeing old friends again.

Preachers were paid very sparingly. Therefore, the congregation was responsible for seeing that someone invited the preacher and his family for Sunday dinner. As part of his salary, he received chickens, vegetables, canned goods, and sometimes baked goods.

Thus, the churches played the role of spiritual guidance, character building, and entertainment.

Eleanore Rowan Moe,
Miner County

Goldie Iron Hawk Takes Her Last Journey

SCHOOL HAD BEEN DISMISSED early the day before in honor of Goldie Iron Hawk, an elder in the community who had passed away, and I decided to attend the funeral. The Iron Hawk people had fought with Crazy Horse at the Little Big Horn. Iron Hawks had ridden with the Hunkpapas and Minneconjous through the Badlands and were with Big Foot at Wounded Knee. Goldie Iron Hawk's

Lakota name was Aena Kiya Pi Win. Her family name was War Bonnet. Her father had been six months old at the Wounded Knee Massacre. His family had escaped and fled, returning to Cheyenne River after the massacre.

The funeral was to begin at eleven in the morning. The little church at Frazier was filled to capacity. As we sat and waited, an older Lakota man began to sing hymns: "How Great Thou Art," "Jesus Loves Me," "The Old Rugged Cross." At times, he would sing the words in Lakota and other times he sang them in English. I noticed the beautiful star quilts hung on the walls and the large piles of quilt top pillows to be given away after the funeral. The pictures, the cakes, and the flowers were all a testament to how much Goldie would be missed. The picture of Jesus and the cross above the casket attested to salvation Goldie had found in the church.

The grandson of Goldie walked in carrying a drum, followed by four of his sons. They began the service with an honor song for their grandmother and great grandmother. Her granddaughter read her obituary. The majority of the service was music. Goldie had loved to sing and to dance. Another granddaughter sang a traditional Lakota song. "I am crying; looking for you. I am crying; looking for you. I am crying; looking for you. I am crying; looking for you." My heart cried with her as she struggled with the words. She had been one of my students my first year teaching. As she sang, I recalled how many of Goldie's grandchildren had been in my classroom as well as nieces, nephews, and cousins.

The music went from gospel to Lakota and back to gospel and then back to Lakota. The speaker kept saying this is a traditional service. Each of the three officiators spoke, and each of them stressed that Jesus was with us and that he would care for us. They spoke with certainty that Goldie had gone to be with her Creator. They spoke in broken English. Lakota words and phrases constantly appeared in their words of encouragement and condolence. "Religion is not only for Christians." Each speaker extolled the importance of accepting Jesus as our Lord and Savior. One speaker spoke of the time when Goldie was saved.   He pointed to the exact pew where she had sat. There was constant movement in the church.   Children running in and out.   Adults walking in and out.   People talking and visiting with friends and relatives who hadn't been seen since the last time there was a funeral in the community. You could see the smoke from the fire pit in the back where they were preparing the traditional buffalo soup.   Food was constantly being carried in whenever anyone new arrived. Young boys were riding horses around outside the church.   I could catch a glimpse of the boys on the horses as they rode past the windows.

The funeral procession was over two miles long. The cemetery was four miles off the main graveled road. The road led through a pasture.   As the procession was making its way to the top of the hill, a painted horse raced up the hill alongside the procession.   When the horse reached the top, he faced the west and stood like a sentinel until the procession had reached the cemetery, and then he turned and faced the south.   The cemetery was in the center at the top of the hill.   Another drum group was present and sang funeral songs while one of Goldie's nephews smudged the crowd and the grave with sweet grass.   As Goldie's grandsons lowered her casket into the grave, the twenty-third Psalm was read, followed by the singing of the four directions prayer song to make the way easier for Aena Kiya Pi Win to make her journey.

Lil Manthei,
Cheyenne River Sioux Reservation

THE LAND

SD State Agricultural Heritage Museum Photographic Collection.

Getting It

IT IS SPRING 2005, my first spring as a South Dakota resident, and we are enjoying early spring warmth. Veronna and I are in the pasture of her family's "old north place." The sun is strong, the meadowlarks and red-winged blackbirds are vocal, and the fresh air is intoxicating to breathe; life is good. The "old north place," near Volga, is the farm Veronna's parents lived on when she was born. To the best of her knowledge, the field we are in has never been cultivated; it is luxuriant with Pasque flowers.

I am not a native South Dakotan. I grew up in Union City, New Jersey. As I unpack my photography gear and listen to the birds, all I can think is how fortunate I am to be here. The largest "field" I saw in my youth was an empty city-sized lot. Now I am standing on prairie not much changed from the way it was when Europeans first came to the Americas. If I climb the pasture's slight hill, I can see for miles to the distant horizon. Yes, life is good.

I am here to photograph Pasque flowers. My first encounter with the Pasque flowers was shortly after Veronna and I married. Every spring, Veronna's mother would send her pressed ones; we were both in the Air Force and in California. I think of the Pasque flower as a beautiful photographic opportunity. I am clueless to the fact that Mom, Veronna, and Gayle see much more. I just do not "get it."

The birds are busy staking territory with their songs. A pair of ducks is taking possession of a small slough. Pheasants are everywhere, calling to each other and forming pairs. Pastures and fields are greening. Life is quickening on the plains; spring is conquering winter. Veronna finds Pasque flowers covering the old pasture's hill.

Now you understand how it is that a city kid, a first generation American son of Italian immigrants and a retired satellite engineer, finds himself in a South Dakota pasture photographing flowers. I am thinking this expedition to the "old north place" is a great "photo op." It becomes much more in my understanding of my new home and its people.

The Pasque flower growth is abundant this year. They are so numerous, I have difficulty not stepping on them, much less choosing which to photograph. I concentrate on my photography, but something else happens. The birds and their singing, the curious cows and new calves in an adjacent pasture, distant farm noises riding the breeze, and the sun's warmth all conspire to transform the moment. I experience an epiphany; I "get it." I understand the flowers' allure and the significance they have for so many people. I appreciate why Mom had to pick and press them for Veronna and why it was valuable for Veronna to get them. These flowers are indeed beautiful, but they are so much more. I comprehend that they are emblematic of spring and the end of a long, dark, cold winter. They are new growth, claiming victory for what will be another season of abundant growth. Regardless of your personal beliefs, you can believe they are vibrant promises of a natural cycle where life triumphs. These flowers are a link between a hardy and trusting people to a land that is both harsh and gracious. The Pasque flowers bring instant memory of growing up and countless springs, and, for the faithful, of a Creator fulfilling His promises.

John T. Capone,
Rural Volga

Prairie Silences

LIVING ON THE LYMAN COUNTY PRAIRIE, we had grown accustomed to the silence that surrounded our farm, silence broken only occasionally by the sound of gears shifting as a car drove down the gravel road just east of us. It was a silence that my father loved, saying there was no use living in the country if you had to hear and see your neighbors across the road; might as well live in town, he said. My mother, however, admired the little clusters of farmhouses we saw from the car windows as we drove east down Highway 16, and she envied the women who lived in those houses, saying it would be nice to hear the comings and goings of other people or to see a neighbor's yard light when she stepped out on the front stoop at night.

Sometimes the silence would be broken by the drone of a car motoring down the dirt road that led to our house, and we would hurry to the front yard to greet our guests. My mother would go into the kitchen, put on a pot of coffee, and squeeze lemon juice into a plastic pitcher with cups of sugar and water and ice. Then she would slice apple pie, chocolate cake, and caramel rolls that always sat on our kitchen counter. Throughout the evening, there would be storytelling and laughter and doors slamming as kids ran in and out of the house.

After a while, my mother would sit at the upright piano and play for the guests who gathered around her singing. I remember Mother playing "Flight of the Bumblebee," her fingers pounding on the keys with such force that she rattled the pictures on the piano's top. This was her grand finale, the signal that the visit was over. Soon after that piano shaking performance, the guests would get into the cars and drive back down the dirt road while Mother stood on the front stoop watching the bright red taillights, the only illumination other than the stars, until their glow faded into the dark and silence descended once again on the farm.

Mary Alice Haug,
Rural Reliance

Windy Mound and the Stone Fence

WE ARE DRIVING EAST on a dusty gravel road into the hills to see the farm where my father grew up. Behind us lie the flats, and just a few miles south, off of State Highway 25, is our new home in Pleasant Valley, next to my paternal grandparents, who are also on the trip.

It is late May 1952. We are in my uncle's new Ford. He is driving. His wife, my Dad's sister, and their two daughters are with us, too. We are crowded into this space together.

Dad tells a story of Grandpa, about how he bought the farm site after seeing it in the gloaming during the winter of 1902. The pasture was filled with small mounds of covered snow. The joke was that Grandpa thought they were resting sheep. Instead, they were just the rocks and boulders that cover the land on these hills. Grandpa chuckles. I cannot tell if he cares about the story.

Rocks and piles of rocks are everywhere. Each spring during thaw, the earth brings up more rocks to the surface. These hills are what remain after thousands of years of glaciers advancing and retreating. One of the last enormous glaciers to advance down from the icy north could not climb over these hills, but split at its northern point. The larger, eastern lobe—the Des Moines lobe—ground its way into Minnesota and Iowa. The western lobe—the James lobe—moved west and south, ironing the soil flat below it. Their combined cold temperature eventually caused the two lobes to grow and meet over the highlands, which extended southward for 200 miles. Finally, about 10,000 years ago, the last glacier receded, carving recesses for water to flow and leaving rich soil, sandy soil, and debris, boulders called erratics, rocks, and giant chunks of ice that would melt in place to become kettle lakes.

Grandpa just laughs, "Well, I made me a good fence out of all them rocks. It took awhile, but I got those fields cleared." He is excited to see it again; he hasn't been up here since they moved to Brookings decades before so the older children could attend college.

The adults keep talking about things in the past. My eyes wander these hills. The road has continued to climb, each small hill followed by another, higher one. Finally, I see a high hill off to the left of the car and ahead.

Grandfather says, "Here. The fence should just be over the hill." We all look to the right to see the fence that Grandfather built from backbreaking rocks.

It takes me a minute to figure out what we are seeing. There are men in the ditch to the right. They are dismantling Grandfather's fence. The adults stop talking, and as the big Ford drives past we all watch the men, who are not smiling as they struggle to loosen the rocks from where they've been sitting for about forty years. None of us are smiling either.

We turn left at the gravel intersection immediately before us, bringing us close to the side of Windy Mound. Harvey drives the car toward the hill, following rutted car tracks slowly and diagonally up the backside of the hill. At the top we stop. The south side is very steep. From there we can see the men still working on the fence. The barn and house at the farm are just a little bit further south from them.

At the top, the women begin setting up a picnic lunch. The wind grabs at the blanket, their skirts, their hats. Marcia and I run down to a lower spot on the north side of the hill. We stand on a huge boulder and have our picture taken. People have carved their names and initials into the rock. Then we turn around and look into North Dakota. Below the hills that lead up to Windy Mound, everything is flat. Miles and miles of flat prairie, as far as the eye can see. I am looking at the edge of the earth; the horizon line seems to curve down at the far edges of the view.

Angela Ilene (Gunderson) Henriksen,
Marshall County

By Greg Latza, Used with permission by Greg Latza.

Learning to Live and Survive: Dry Land Farming in the West River

MY FATHER TOLD ME STORIES of the Depression, wind, drought, loss of a farm, moving back and forth between town and farm. When I decided to ranch on a small scale, all of my anxieties were stimulated. Standing at the kitchen window with a pair of binoculars, I would watch a cow try to give birth. As the time went from thirty minutes to forty-five to an hour, my anxiety grew and pacing would increase. Off I went to help out. This, I learned, interfered with survival, because if I moved too quickly to intervene it would really upset the mother cow. It could lead to a dead calf just as well as if I waited too long. Soon I learned the subtle signs and became a better judge of time and a more patient person.

Farming was in my blood, so I rented a piece of land to grow hay and barley. It would teach me that patience is not the only virtue. Early in a rather wet spring we planted barley in strips that alternated with existing hay, giving the barley some wind protection. There is that wonderful feeling of accomplishment seeing the clean strips of worked black earth contrasting with the green of the emerging wheat grass alfalfa strips. We finished and then I waited. Just let it grow. But to our chagrin, it soon rained a few inches with West River ferocity, straight down. It was over in thirty minutes, followed by a clearing blue sky. Out to the field I went the next day to check things out, only to see ruts and washouts. Clearly, we had to replant, and so we did as soon as the field dried out. Then, after a few more gentle rains and the hint of green coming on, it turned bone dry and the faucet was off. Holy cow, I wondered how long before it would rain again. Things still came up and hope did spring eternal in spite of an early summer drought. Looking to the west, we hoped for rain and got it. But along with it hail pounded and leveled the barley and cut to shreds the wheat grass and alfalfa. But by golly I was still patient, anxious but patient. Then, right before harvest, the dryness brought the locusts. Grasshoppers, hungry for whatever was in their way, decimated what was left. Yet my patience did not waiver, and harvest I would. So we windrowed and combined and got four bushels an acre.

Sitting there in the pickup after checking the production, I laughed. And after laughing I felt better. I thought this should make great lyrics for a country western song—from rain to drought to hail to grasshoppers; you could cry but you have to laugh. Well, nobody sings it, but I learned that patience and persistence needed humor for survival.

Gerald Mohatt,
Todd County

Sledding on Dirt Drifts

"THAT DRIFT IS TOTALLY BROWN! Daddy, can I go sledding on that drift?"

The wind was blowing—not just blowing, but a gale. It was loaded with particles of prairie dirt. The precious topsoil from my father's alfalfa field was rapidly forming drifts in the ditches. I was just a tyke and thought all drifts were made for sledding. My dad told me that these drifts were made of just dirt and that my sled would not work on them. I was very disappointed but even more upset by the look on my dad's face when he explained what these drifts meant to our family.

It was the middle of a long, dry summer. What few crops we had were rapidly burning up in the fields or had already succumbed to the heat and drought. The wind blew non-stop and eroded our precious topsoil into the ditches. Dad said that this topsoil could not be replaced for years. Rain alone could not repair all this damage.

Being young and innocent, I decided I could help my dad. I got out my favorite toy bucket and shovel and started loading up that topsoil into my little red wagon and proceeded to haul it back on the field.

My dad could not refrain from smiling and then grabbed his shovel and helped me load my wagon. We worked silently side by side until we were exhausted. At least, I know I was exhausted.

The drought continued for two more years, but my dad and I always cherished the day we worked together to save our topsoil.

Kay Smeenk,
Rural Box Elder

On Finding Home

WHEN I WAS A KID, I thought the world ended just beyond 218 NelTom Drive, my grandparents' house in Pierre, South Dakota. I could stand on my tiptoes there, peer into the distance, and see only edges of blue sky and blanched earth. I thought if I wandered out beyond those small hillocks I would be lost forever, that with my light hair and pale skin, I'd fade into the toneless plain and I'd be rooted there like some fabled prairie gnome among the sputtering grackles and lonesome coyotes.

The land was frightening; it was worn and sparse. The summer sun threatened to devour whole fields of soybeans and sunflowers, while the winters imposed frigid air and howling winds. It was, and is, a land that demands respect. And it is a land that takes as much as it gives. I've since lived east and west of the Missouri River, but though I've had chances, I've not left my home state. What I have learned during my life here is that this is my land, as bleak as it sometimes may seem. My grandparents' families came here from Norway and settled in, most as farmers. They changed their inflected Nordic surnames to ones that matched the level, comfortable dialect of the Midwest. No one can remember our homeland names; no one can remember who we were before we were South Dakotans. That's how deep the land runs in our blood.

The stories run there, too. My grandfather Huse's memories are a lifetime's worth of snapshots of central South Dakota:

Of his dad, left three-fingered after trying to clear a jam in the corn sheller—

Of saving a piece of bread every day for the lambs on his walk home from school—

Of Christmas and how the candles looked so nice on the tree until the fire happened—

Of Ma Money and her liquor shack next to the pool hall—

Of living in the coffin room of a funeral home during business school—

Of the dance halls in Harrold and Murdo and Agar—

Of lighting corn cobs on fire in the winter to heat the oil tank of the Pontiac—

Of leaving on the Galloping Goose, the caboose carrying the servicemen out of town—

Of how farming was too hard of work back then with the shovel, pick, and crowbar—

Of how times were tough back then, but they don't seem much better now—

Of how there was never a question of living anywhere else.

I realize now that what frightened me when I was a kid was the vastness of this land and its power to take away. Years later, I find that it makes no secret of its power to give as well. Beyond the history and memories tied to this landscape, there is beauty here. You'll find it in the lustrous amber of spring wheat and the sunflowers' easy worship of the sun. Glimpse it in a nine-combine harvest or a deep summer rain. Find it in the long steady V of the Canada geese in flight, or their peaceful current drifting down the Missouri. Observe it in the stealth of the nighttime scavengers: the masked raccoons, the black-jacketed skunk families, and the pink-faced opossums that live off oddments of land and lives. Witness a doe and her fawn grazing at dusk and you'll know why I stay. For me, I find it in the early morning hours standing on the back deck of my parents' place in Spearfish Canyon. It's in the rustling echo of sixty wild turkeys, podgy and ragged, trudging down the back hill of the golf course towards the oak tree just beyond the step. Even after I leave them for the warmth of the fireplace, I'll hear them for an hour or more, scratching and scratching the ground beneath the feeders where the Nuthatches and Blue Jays spilled yesterday's seed. They, too, know the secrets of this land. This is when I truly grasp what lies beyond the edges of sky, and I think it wouldn't be so bad to find myself lost here.

Courtney Huse Wika,
Pierre and Spearfish

WEATHER AND SEASONS

SD State Agricultural Heritage Museum Photographic Collection.

Dirty Thirties

WE WOULD WATCH THE WORST STORMS roll in from the west from our vantage point on our farm near Aurora. They could strike at any time of day or night, but usually hit in early or late afternoon. They were most frequent during 1935 and 1936, varying in intensity and occurring two to three times a month during June, July, and August of those years. Our warning would be a growing accumulation of dark clouds along the western horizon that rolled horizontally across the prairie. A distant roar would increase in volume as the clouds neared the farm, bringing with them a unique taste identifiable as dust.

As the clouds rolled and churned our way, our immediate task was to run through the farmyard and close the barn doors, shoo chickens into the chicken house before closing its doors, and get the horses and other livestock out of the barn. If the barn were to collapse, the livestock would be safer outdoors than in. After shutting off the windmill, to prevent the violent winds from spinning the fan until it tore off the system, we scurried into the cellar. These chores were automatic. No one needed to be told what to do or when to do it.

The noise was frightful and was made worse by the sound of tree trunks and limbs snapping and the shudder of the house as it stood up to the wind. Nevertheless, we felt safe, huddled together in the darkness of the narrow passage. The storms brought no rain or lightning, just dust carried on the ferocious wind. They were over in a matter of minutes, whereupon we emerged from the cellar and surveyed the damage. Among the debris would be parts of trees and buildings scattered across the farmyard. Often a corncrib or outbuilding would be capsized or blown down.

During one of the worst mid-afternoon storms, the sun was completely obscured, limiting our visibility to barely a few feet. Pop was somewhere in the field with the horses, and we headed for the cellar without him, deeply concerned. After the storm, we were greatly relieved to find him in the farmyard with the horses. He explained that the horses instinctively found their way back, bringing him with them.

The house had no insulation, and its structure was not weathertight enough to ward off the penetrating dust. It came in through cracks around the edges of windows and doors and through the siding of buildings. Sand and grit found its way into food, and our mouths were always grainy with it. It drifted like snow along fencerows and in some spots completely covered fences and posts. Crops were decimated. Wind and blowing sand cut down the few plants that survived the drought. The only vegetation that resisted the elements was Russian thistle, or tumbleweed, which, fortunately, had some feed value. During the worst years, we stacked it as hay.

Norman D. Thomsen,
Rural Brookings

Fighting Grasshoppers in the 1930s

YELLOWS, PINKS, AND REDS in the western sky cast through the haze as the sun dipped near the horizon. Welcome relief from 100-degree heat came to the Cheyenne River valley that was our home. The late 1930s found the Joe and Vera Lytle family battling the odds of survival on this sand-blown, wind-swept farm four-and-a-half miles northwest of Wasta.

Dad worked tirelessly in the sweltering heat to keep his balky Twin City tractor running and prevent it from overheating at the irrigation pump station. The huge flywheel kept a thirty-foot-long heavy canvas belt turning that ran the pump and lifted the eight-inch stream of water up into the big irrigation ditch. He kept us girls busy with half-filled buckets of wet poison bran and a piece of shingle to slop the mash along the big irrigation ditch at the end of the garden and long corn rows. The greedy grasshoppers ate readily of their sweet death. Brothers Joe and Larry, much younger, weren't allowed near the poison bran barrel. It was worry enough for Dad to give us girls this dangerous job, he knowing that devilment of my sister Lyla, just two years older than I. He didn't need an extra worry of two little boys who might carelessly slop the poison on themselves. Dead grasshoppers piled one and two inches deep along the ditches and in the corn rows were warning enough of its deadliness.

As welcome dusk swallowed the lengthening shadows, intense rolling heat waves disappeared. Brothers Joe and Larry would now get their turn fighting hoppers. Mama reminded, "Get the old shirt and sacks from the porch; it's time to drive hoppers out before dark." Dad, Mama, and we six kids spread out across the big garden and sweetcorn field. We swished the shirts and sacks beneath plants and through corn, flushing out hordes of the greedy creatures. They flew toward the fence lines, now too dark to move back into their haven of eating. After several sweeps we managed to drive out most of them that were intent upon gobbling up our livelihood. Only three- and four-inch wingless grasshoppers remained. Each morning, we rejoiced at the many lying on their backs, their legs twitching for a last time after feasting the night on poison bran.

Dad believed that grasshoppers did most of their feeding at night. His theory must have been true, for during the grasshopper-infested 1930s we managed to save most of our garden and corn when our neighbors' bigger commercial gardens were nearly stripped. Our good neighbor John Hays said many times in his tight-lipped English brogue, "Joe, I never seed the likes of how yous fight 'dem hoppers. I don't know how yous do it." Without half a dozen hard-working, capable kids, Dad and Mama would never have accomplished such a near impossible task.

Onalee Lytle Hoffman,
Pennington County

Coping During the "Dirty Thirties"

THE FIRST BAD DROUGHT that I can remember was in 1930 or 1931. I remember that we quit cultivating corn after it got so dry. The drought continued strong for the next six years. It dried out the soil so bad that wherever you walked a cloud of dust sprang up. Finally, the dust storms arrived. We had a lot of windy days in the summer. When we were cultivating, we could hardly see forward. Some days we could not even see the sun. It was almost dark during the afternoon. After the wind went down, piles of dust like snowdrifts were left behind. Sometimes the drifts were as high as three feet. We could just see a little of the fence posts. In some places, cows could actually walk over the fences. The dust also buried machinery, and sometimes, whole buildings.

The grasshoppers just about destroyed all of the crops. They would seem to come almost overnight. We would notice a few hoppers and pretty soon there would be thousands of them. They would eat practically everything out of our fields. They would eat paint off the house and barn, too. Sometimes they even ate fence posts completely. Grasshoppers would cover posts so we couldn't actually see the post. We would just see the outline of it. Grasshoppers also got into the house and into our food. When we went to the store in town, there would be grasshoppers everywhere. One time I helped a neighbor drive some cattle to Platte. On the way, I noticed that I could count the stalks of corn in a field. The grasshoppers had eaten practically everything in it. We tried to kill the grasshoppers by a poisonous mash. I think we got the mash from the government. We spread that mash with an end gate seeder. We also put the mash on posts where the hoppers slept. We put it on early in the morning. It helped a little, but not much.

To feed our cattle during the Depression, we raised some grain, and we also received some from the government. We also used Russian thistles for feed. This seemed to be the only thing that the grasshoppers didn't eat. Russian thistles were round, grassy bushes. We cut them when they were green and before they got sticky. We fed this to the livestock like hay. Russian thistles would also grow in our grain fields. Every spring before we plowed the field, we would rake the thistles together and set fire to them. Sometimes the fire would get out of hand, and we would have to get the neighbors to help put it out.

Louis Niehus, Deceased
Geddes
Submitted by Ron Dufek

Blizzard of 1986

BLIZZARDS COME WITH THE TERRITORY when you live in South Dakota, but normally they do not arrive in April. The April 1986 blizzard is one our family will long remember.

The Sunday, April 13, 1986, weather report was forecasting a winter storm and predicting eight inches of snow. How could this be when just the day before we had planted a few things in the garden? But during the children's sermon at church, while the minister was showing the kids crocus and tulips bulbs, large snowflakes started falling outside. By the time we arrived home from church, my husband and his brothers were moving the cattle into several lots around the home place, just west and north of the house. One group was behind the shelterbelt near the bale stacks and another was near the barn. Hayracks, truck, and trailers were moved in as windbreaks.

As the snow and strong winds continued throughout the day, about a dozen cows had their calves. At two a.m. on April 14, my husband and I bundled up to check the cattle by the barn. It was impossible to see anything, and the snow felt like grains of sand hitting our faces. Before going out in the storm, I drew a large footprint on several sheets of paper. These were laid on the kitchen floor leading to the basement. The children, Mark, 6, Nathan, 4, and Andrea, 2, were sleeping, and I wanted them to follow the footprints, if they awoke, and find the baby calves.

Two of my husband's brothers called at six a.m. They were unable to make it to the farm. The winds were forty to fifty mph, and the wind chill factor was twenty to thirty degrees below zero. That day was spent battling the snow and trying to rescue calves. On one trip to the barn we discovered our cat "Digger" with three new baby kittens. I put the kittens in an old metal bucket, caught the mother cat, and took them all back to the house. Now we had both baby calves and baby kittens in the house!

We used our horse "Sundown" to help drag calves through the snow. As the storm continued, he became covered with snow and his eyes iced over. Dragging calves through the snow and lifting them over fences in miserable conditions were very exhausting for the horse and for us. The baby calves were taken to the basement, where the kids tried to dry them off with my hairdryer. For our efforts, we saved some of the calves but many died. By afternoon there were huge snowdrifts everywhere, and Sundown refused to go through them. In places, the drifts were as high as the bale stacks, and some of the cows had gone over the fences.

The blizzard was finally over Tuesday morning, leaving deep snow banks behind. The guys worked all day, moving cows and trying to put cow and calf pairs back together. At week's end, it was estimated that forty to forty-five calves died. Throughout the ordeal, there were fourteen different calves in the house basement. The kids thought it was fun, and Nathan picked out a black whiteface to "take to the county fair."

North of the house, the drifts in the trees were twelve to fifteen feet high. The snowdrifts near the old shop feathered all the way across the farmyard, south to the road and headed towards the neighbor's home a quarter-mile away. The garden that we planted on Saturday was completely buried under snow, but it did eventually come up!

It was one blizzard we will never forget!

Kathleen Nagel,
Potter County

Boy in Slough

IT WAS THE SUMMER OF 1938 in the southeastern pot hole prairie land of Miner County, South Dakota, and at last there was hope. At least that's what the eight-year-old boy overheard. There had been a little snow the winter before and a few quick showers that spring and summer. Not a lot, but some. There was enough moisture to be optimistic.

They'd planted sorghum because it was known to have drought-resistant qualities. Besides, they could use all the plant could produce. The seed would feed chickens. They'd chop the stalks and make feed for the cattle. Corn cobs would have been really nice for the cook stove, but those were a luxury. Cattails and slough grass were twisted for use in the stove ever since he could remember anyway.

It all depended on the rain. He could count the rains that had happened before he went to school. He'd be in the third grade this coming fall in the country school a half mile from his home. He attended there with thirty-two other kids in grades one through eight—most of them now third generation immigrants to Dakota Territory.

But school was a few weeks off yet and everybody was needed to tend to the sorghum crop. It had a chance to make it. Weeding went on for weeks, by hand, up and down the rows. It was hot. It was dusty. He thought that was the way it always was.

He'd walk home close to dark, cutting through the slough. It was really hot and dusty there with the slough grasses growing high, except for where they'd cut them for fuel. He wondered about why they didn't plant sorghum there when they did on the hill behind the slough. He loved running through the slough to the top of the hill. From there you could see to forever.

One day was different. Everything seemed taut and expectant. The air hummed and even the birds and bugs seemed excited. Dad said it looked like a big rain could be coming. Maybe, maybe. At eight years old he'd never seen one.

That evening, his mom warned about being too close to the window. You never knew when the wind might put a branch through it. Lightning was a scary thing; a neighbor boy had been killed riding his horse to school a few years ago.

But he had to see and smell rain just once. Thunder and lightning and the wind had a voice all their own. He could see it coming for miles. The storm looked as big up and down as it did across. Rain. Five inches of rain. It was a miracle. It filled up the slough, something he'd never seen before. He just had to go out the next morning and check it all out. It was a new place and a new time. He was a part of it all. Dad said he'd done a good job and wasn't it lucky they had worked so hard before the rain came. Mom said she would take a picture of him because he had worked so hard, as hard as any man could. He smiled from ear to ear as he rolled up his coveralls and ran into the water. He was a product of these plains. He knew the seasons there, the creatures, the insects, the moods of the hours with sky and land. He knew he had what it took in tough times. He'd remember this lesson for always. He'd never forget this summer of work and weeds and wonder. It was his prairie home.

Kathryn Stangohr Callies,
Miner County

South Dakota Snowstorm

JOHN KUIPER HAD BEEN AN APPRENTICE PAINTER in the Netherlands. While living in New Holland he and his brother Herman got a job to paint a house in Harrison, a town four miles east. After walking to Harrison, they boarded there for one week. This was in March or April, around 1920. On Saturday, they decided to walk home to spend Sunday at home. They began the four-mile walk, but it soon began to snow, and a full-blown snow storm developed. After a time, they found a straw or hay stack to rest in. John wanted to stay, but Herman said they would freeze to death. So they continued west, following a fence until they came to the Brower place one mile east of New Holland. The Browers put up John and Herman over Saturday night. Sunday morning, the brothers walked the mile to New Holland. They had nearly frozen. John slept straight through till Tuesday.

Chester VanderZee,
Douglas County

Record Snow Falls

MY FATHER, EUGENE KILBRIDE, remembers the winter of 1936 as a ten-year-old boy living on a farm near Wakonda. "It got like 20 degrees below zero and it snowed for six weeks and nobody even had school and we had snow drifts six feet deep," he recalled. Grandma Rose resorted to killing her chickens to feed the family because they ran out of meat and supplies.

Eugene witnessed two more record snow falls. During the winter of 1964-65, while he was living on a farm northwest of Wakonda with his wife and twelve children, the snow was so deep that they could touch the telephone lines between the house and barn. "Dad kept the cows in the barn because he couldn't get them out, and we crawled in through a tunnel in the snow to help milk them," said daughter Pat Anderson. The snow plow carved a tunnel through the snow on the road. The following summer, a hail storm produced hail the size of shooter marbles. The girls were caught in it as they herded the cows in from the field. The cows were jumping and kicking, and the girls put their hands over their heads.

The year of 1968-69, while Dad was living on a farm southeast of Wakonda, it began snowing the weekend after Thanksgiving and continued every weekend for weeks, until drifts reached the height of twenty feet. Snow plows quit trying to keep the roads open. School was held for students who could reach the paved roads. His children walked a mile one way to meet the school bus on the blacktop south of the farm. Daughters Jeannie and Gloria spent some weeks in town with family friends so they would be able to get enough credits to complete the school year.

A collie dog named Laddie stayed in the milk parlor near the space heater, and Siamese tom cat Tommy slept on the foot of the girls' beds. Snow was scooped off the Quonset to keep it from collapsing. Cows had trails in the yard. Hay bales were frozen solid from rain that fell prior to the snow fall. They had to be pried apart with crowbars before they could be broken apart and fed to the cows. Milk from the dairy barn had to be dumped down the drain because the milk truck couldn't make it to the farm to pump the milk out of the bulk tank.

Daughter Joie and husband Terry Pickett brought the family groceries from Vermillion on a snowmobile. The meat supply ran low and son Daniel was sent into the tree grove north of the farm to shoot rabbits for supper. Eugene's wife Irene rolled them in flour and fried them like chicken. Son Mike became ill with a bronchial infection, and Eugene had to walk a mile to the blacktop to meet a vehicle so he could be driven to Vermillion for medical care.

When the spring thaw arrived, five-foot icicles hung from the eves of the house, as the snow sitting on top of the house began to melt. The ditches were filled dangerously high with melting snow, which flooded many of the roads. Whirlpools of swirling water sucked through the overburdened culverts. Eugene warned his children to stay a long ways away for fear they'd be sucked in and drowned.

Gloria Bauske,
Wakonda

A Shot in the Dark

FLORENCE #3 WAS A RURAL SCHOOL in Hamlin County on Highway 81 between Watertown and Hayti, located on the bend about halfway between the two towns. The year was 1946. My name was Lillian Halonen, eighteen years of age. I taught in that school for two years. I had thirteen pupils. The school was a large, white, boxy school with a full basement. Our county superintendent was Doris Boadwine.

In January of that year, we had a major snowstorm. It was Wednesday, a golden, wintry morning. I had breakfast with Mavis Junso. She fixed a box lunch and I was off for the half-mile trek to the school. I fixed up the banked fire in the furnace, checked my plans, and made ready for the day. Soon, kids began to arrive. Mrs. Kemp brought a cream can filled with water for the porcelain water jug. It was nine and time for opening exercises. About noon, the wind began to howl. We pulled down the shades facing north and they would move along with the wind. I was a bit wary about the increasing darkness and the intensity of the wind as the room was getting cold. By this time, the snow had started and we could sense the blizzard. There was no way we were leaving that building! By three, it was very dark. The building seemed to shake. We put on our coats and kept feeding the furnace. The furnace room was in the basement. We did have plenty of coal, and the kids thought it was all great fun!

We heard the outer door open, and "klomping" up the stairs was Mr. Garner, covered with snow! He had hitched up a team of horses to a wagon, but he could not take anyone home. He barely made it to the school. However, he had a bucket of sandwiches, and he told us to stay at the school until help arrived. He also brought a kerosene lantern. We had our coats; we had light; we had food. It was warm. We huddled around the floor furnace and told stories and sang! We made beds around the floor furnace, because it was cold if we moved beyond this source of heat. Richard Kemp, one of the students, and I made many trips to the furnace room to shovel in more coal. Using the lantern, I could see the beady eyes of mice as they scurried in the coal bin.

About midnight, we were startled to hear a sharp bang, right under our noses—an explosive sound. During this confusion, Richard explained that he had a rifle bullet in his coat pocket. Evidently, it had slipped into the furnace itself and exploded! I was never so happy for a lantern! It was dark, it was scary, but somehow this teacher held it together, and daylight arrived and the storm raged on. Mr. Garner came back with some parents that day, and Florence #3 dismissed school that week!

Lillian Hand,
Hamlin County

Safe At Home

THESE DAYS I GET TO TRAVEL SOME and see a good deal of the countryside. Whenever I pass an abandoned farmstead, I can't help but feel a twinge of sadness. I will look at the old barn—perhaps it has sagged into a pile of weathering lumber, its timbers exposed like the ribs of a colossal wooden dinosaur—and think of all the animals it sheltered in years gone by.

The decaying house might sit in a patch of weeds, its empty windows like the blank eye sockets of a weathered skull. I will look at its deserted rooms and know that laughter once rang through this now unkempt building, this forlorn place that someone once called "home." Babies came into the world within its warm confines, and wakes were held for departed loved ones in its parlor.

The fields surrounding the farmstead are now farmed with the ruthless efficiency that has become the mantra of modern agriculture. Once upon a time, what is now a single large field that grows a single crop was divided into several smaller fields. Each spring, its former owner debated over what to plant in these fields. Was that bottomland too wet for alfalfa? Would it be a good year for wheat? Maybe that field north of the trees should be planted to silage corn. All of this has been replaced by a single swipe of an enormous implement that sows the seeds and applies a variety of chemicals that will all but guarantee a good yield while allowing the farmer to pay almost no attention to the land.

Seeing an abandoned farmstead always reminds me of a near-calamity that befell Dad when he was a schoolboy. One winter, a powerful blizzard swept down upon the prairie, howling across the plains like the horsemen of the Apocalypse. Dad and his schoolmates found themselves trapped at their small, one-room schoolhouse out in the middle of the country. Coal and other supplies were short.

The roar of the blizzard was abruptly interrupted by a sound at the door. It was my Grandpa, who announced that he had come to take the children to safety. Grandpa herded the kids into a wagon box he had mounted on his bobsled. Dad said he was surprised when, after he had secured a hay tarp over his human cargo, Grandpa joined them in the wagon box. Grandpa then lifted a front corner of the tarp and barked "Getup!" at his team of giant Belgians.

Dad said it was eerie. The only sounds in the wagon box were the howl of the wind and jangle of the harnesses. The bobsled suddenly ground to a halt. Grandpa clambered out and used his pliers to cut the barbed wire fence that had stopped the team. Grandpa then resumed his spot in the wagon box and again barked at the team to "Getup!"

Dad related that at one point he peeked out from under the hay tarp. The air was so thick with snow that it seemed as if God were shaking out the contents of a cosmic feather pillow; the drifts were belly deep to the Belgians, forcing them to make great bounding leaps. The powerful animals lunged in perfect unison, the hallmark of an excellent team.

Dad said that Grandpa had to get out and cut the fence a second time, but that when the team stopped for the third time, they were standing outside their barn door. The kids joined hands and made their way through the swirling snow to the house. Dad said that he glanced back and saw Grandpa pressing his forehead against the forehead of one of the Belgians, giving the mighty beast silent thanks for the safe delivery of this dearest of all cargoes.

Jerry Nelson,
Volga

Making Do at Christmas

THAT YEAR, 1951, was a pretty lean year on our family farm. We were, by today's standards, a fairly large family—Mom, Daddy, and four children. Of course, as a small child, I was unaware of my parents' financial concerns. My older sister was nine years old. The rest of us were two, three, and four years old. Little did we know, Mom and Daddy had heavy hearts because there was little cash left over that December to provide Christmas for "the wee ones." To make matters worse, it had snowed hard and the roads in rural Bennett County of Central South Dakota were closed.

My Mom, Charlotte Wallingford, was always very resourceful and innovative. This "Christmas crisis" in 1951 was yet another challenge for Mom. She assessed what supplies she had to work with and set to work "creating." Mom told of staying up all night for several nights after putting us kids to bed, sewing new doll clothes from brightly printed flour sacks for my older sister's doll. My younger sister and I were the doting owners of rubber "baby" dolls. Mom painted their hair black and sewed new diapers, receiving blankets, and kimonos from worn out, recycled, flannel pajamas for our cherished "babies." So far, so good!

Mom's last task was to design and construct something from materials on hand for my little brother, Riley, then two years old. Riley was a toddler, just walking good. Mom took an old broomstick, some leather, yarn, straw (plentiful on the farm), paint, and upholstery tacks and made Riley the most magnificent stick horse any of us had ever seen. I do believe Riley cherished that stick horse almost as much as Roy Rogers loved his horse, Trigger.

Mom and Daddy had a house full of very happy little ones that Christmas morning in 1951. We were not poor by any standard that Christmas morning so long ago, and none of us had any complaints about our hand-made Christmas gifts. Well, I

guess Riley did have one teeny, tiny comment. He wondered why
his horse didn't have stirrups.

Billee Schaible,
Rural Vetal

This Was Christmas

The one time in the year
our whole rural community
used to gather together was Christmas
at our one-room country schoolhouse.
Seems as though everyone had
at least one child in school.
Our program was rehearsed for weeks in advance.
Each of us had our part
in skits and Christmas songs.
We would hang up blankets suspended
from a wire strung wall-to-wall
making curtains for our stage.
Names were drawn and
every schoolmate would receive a gift.
Scissor-cut paper snowflakes and
Frosty the Snowman danced across
the school's windowpanes and walls.
Then, on the last day of school before vacation,
planks from outside were brought in

and placed between two desk seats to provide
seating for parents.
We would come back in the evening
to a schoolhouse all lit up,
and pile our heavy coats
on the corner library table.
We kids would hide in the wings of our
blanket-curtained stage, waiting for our cues,
and then say our lines earnestly, with smiles.
A white-whiskered, red-suited Santa
always showed up just at the end of the last song
with peanuts, chocolates, and candy canes.
In the pictures, we were wearing our best,
our mothers and fathers were young,
and our faces shone with an inner light.

> *Bruce Roseland,*
> *Faulk County*

Christmas on the Farm

QUART JARS FILLED WITH COINS were what remained from weekly allowances for the purpose of buying gifts for Christmas. It was the only time of the year that fruit was bought, and a box of red delicious apples sat on the kitchen table. A tree adorned with translucent glass balls filled the living room with the scent of pine and our hearts with the spirit of Christmas.

One Christmas in the mid-1950s, we visited Grandpa and Grandma Kilbride on their twenty-acre farm north of Wakonda. The smell of cinnamon-laced apple butter, intertwined with coffee, stimulated my appetite. After the meal I walked through the barn. Leather collars once worn by the plow horses hung on the wall, and the smell of horse sweat permeated them. A tree grove across the road from the acreage was a haven for rabbits and birds that hid in the briar patches that scratched our limbs as we picked bittersweet.

The horses had been replaced by a John Deere tractor in the early 1960s. I jiggled across the field in the spring shortly after the birds returned, and the thawing earth tickled my nose like pepper. The oats and clover between my toes itched and soothed my feet as Grandpa and I sowed oats and clover with a seeder wagon. A chain attached to the back wagon axle and the seeder box made it spin, broadcasting the seed. Dad followed us with a John Deere tractor and a single-section disc.

The oats, straw, and alfalfa filled the barn loft in winter months. A pulley once used to hoist it up by the wagon loads with the help of horses was no longer used in the 1960s. We grabbed the ropes and swung the entire length of the barn for fun. A trap door in the loft opened into a grain bin in the lower corner of the barn.

After Catechism on Saturday mornings, I bought root beer at the drug store. We drove to Yankton to shop in the big department stores. The narrow highway wound like Christmas ribbon through farmland scattered with stacks of hay and gray trails in the snow that looked like tinsel strewn about the farmyards, where trucks and tractors had made their way in the fluffy, white snow. Smoke curled from chimneys, colliding with the cold Dakota skyline.

The Saturday after Thanksgiving, Santa Claus visited the town of Wakonda in a fire truck that parked on Main Street. Bags filled with hard candy, peanuts, and an apple were handed to the waiting hands of children, as the joyous sound of Santa's Ho! Ho! Ho! sent our hearts racing.

A pot of oyster stew awaited our return from midnight mass at the St Patrick's Catholic Church in Wakonda on Christmas Eve, as cars crunched through the snow, coming to rest in parking spots near the church. At the end of Father McMahon's sermon, candles were lit for the candle-light vigil. It had a somber ending and we left the church with the true meaning of Christmas renewed within us.

Cows lowed in the Quonset, and snowflakes shined like prisms in the beam of the yard light. The sparkling lights of the Christmas tree in the window brought me back to the present day Christmas, and the anticipation of what tomorrow morning would bring thrilled me through and through.

Gloria Bauske,
Wakonda

ON THE FARM

SD State Agricultural Heritage Museum Photographic Collection.

Harvest Time

I ALWAYS KNEW HARVEST TIME WAS GETTING CLOSER when Dad took us for a ride through the fields after church every Sunday. We would admire the oats, wheat, barley, and flax as we drove slowly through the farmland. Dad would proudly state when this field had been planted and when it would probably be harvested.

This was an exciting but tense time in our lives, living on a farm northeast of Aberdeen. I was fortunate to have brothers who helped Dad with the harvest as well as hired men whom Dad hired every year. However, I did have a purpose and I could be of help!

When the crops were ready to harvest, someone had to take lunch out to the men at 3:00. This meant we made sandwiches, cookies, and lemonade for their break. They would take a break, relax, and talk about how much work they had finished that day. It was a huge step when I could finally drive the car by myself to take them their lunch. I had to drive over a big hill that had a railroad running over it. I was always nervous it would tear the bottom of the car out while I was crossing it. Later, as an adult, I drove to that place and realized that big hill was barely a bump!

Dad would take the time to show us how to make wheat gum by chewing the wheat until it turned to gum. That was a big treat. It made me feel happy to see Dad laugh and have fun.

On the way home from bringing the lunch we would stop at the tree claim to check the plums. If some were ripe, we would pick them to make jelly later.

It was a great harvest meal every evening, as Mom would fry chicken and make gravy and mashed potatoes. She would slice plates of fresh tomatoes from the garden and make cucumbers with cream and vinegar. Mom always had cookies, pie, or canned fruit for dessert. I remember snapping beans and podding peas on the swing on the front porch while waiting for Dad to arrive for this delicious deal.

My dad used to tell me that farmers were the biggest gamblers in the world. I could sense that as we watched storm clouds come up in a hurry and worry about hail and storm damage.

Finally, harvest time would be over and life seemed calm and more secure for all of us. We would then go on a vacation to Wyoming or Wisconsin.

Vonnie Karlen Shields,
Brown County

Cutting Silage

I WAS RAISED ON A FARM in the rural Bryant area. Every fall around State Fair time was also silage-cutting time. Neighbors would come together just as they did in the threshing days. One farmer would have the tractor and cutter; others would have a tractor pulling a wagon, moving from farm to farm.

When we were young, perhaps too young to help, people anticipated, with great expectation, when is the crew coming here? One of the fun times was mealtime, being able to listen to the talk of what farmers talked about in those days. That was before Mom scooted us out of the way. Maybe she didn't want us to hear what they were saying! Another fun thing for us in the evening, when all the neighbors went home to do their own chores, was checking out all the tractors, comparing the neighbors' Internationals to Dad's John Deeres. It seemed the M's went faster than the A's.

The ultimate fun thing was playing on the silage pile. A little imagination went a long way. We were allowed to do this for a few days, until the fermenting process started. Then Dad had better not see any footprints on the pile!

Another memory of silage was the sound of a forkful of silage coming down the chute of the silo. One could always tell how fast one of my brothers was working, or they me! The smell of silage to this day still triggers these fond memories!

At that time of my life, I thought it must be great being a town kid. Now, I am thankful I was a country kid.

Larry Noem,
Rural Bryant

Aromatherapy, Country Style

SO MANY OF THE THINGS WE TAKE FOR GRANTED can come back to our memories in mere moments, triggered by the sense of smell. When I was little we raised sheep. Most of my thoughts about them are that they butted me and tried to knock the five-gallon buckets full of shelled corn out of my hands when I fed them. I remember shearing time and the ticks while stomping wool in the huge gunnysacks. Last year, while visiting with other ranch wives, one mentioned KRS, an insecticide that is no longer used on sheep. I could smell it! I hadn't thought of it in years, but the memory of that odor was ingrained.

For five years we had a Grade A dairy. A salesman talked us into trying a product for odor control. Actually it did mask the dairy odor with a sickeningly sweet cherry based smell. I believe the name was Odie Granules. Some derivative of it is still around and occasionally I get a whiff of it. Then I'm right back in the dairy barn.

Diesel fumes? Though common in the country, they transport me back to my college days when I studied at the University of Paris, the Sorbonne, in France. The city buses were numerous, and they spewed their exhausts in the face. Funny thing is, until the fumes were so concentrated, I never noticed them. Now, they bring back memories.

The scent I love the most is newly cut alfalfa hay. It is indescribable. Figure out a way to bottle that smell and you would be a millionaire many times over. The market would be for anyone who ever lived in the country or would like to do so. Think of all the retired farmers who experienced the fragrance and their grandchildren who haven't, and the many of the generation in between who have had to leave their farms.

Two nights ago I awoke to the strangest smell and had to think about what it was. It has been a long time since we had enjoyed the aroma of rain. Even the scent of rain gives hope to farmers, and with the southern Black Hills just to the west, whiffs are often all we get. Two-tenths doesn't do a lot for the soil, but it does wonders for the air and for the soul.

Peggy Sanders,
Rural Oral
Previously published in "The Rocky Mountain Fence Post"

These Old Tractors

These old tractors still beller their innards
to the sky.
The two-, four-, the six-cylinder
work horses that won't die.
Paint faded, scraped and dented,
with half the instrument panel dead.
Bare-wired, rattled tin and all
still doing the odd jobs.
When you sit on a tractor
for forty-odd years
it's the same as having a friend
that you cuss at.
Where would we be without
the Case, the I.H., the John Deere
and the Moline?
The young men would rather sit
in the ones with the cab
and stay clean.
But I would just as soon
cut the backlots' weeds
sitting on the old one
with my memories.

Bruce Roseland,
Faulk County

Field Lunch

EVERY KID GROWING UP on a small farm in 1960s South Dakota knew the four standard meals of a working day: breakfast, dinner, lunch, and supper. Coming from Norwegian, or some Scandinavian ancestral mix, our mothers made sure that hard-working men were well fed. I figure one reason God gave these hearty folks children was to go fetch the men out of the field when it was time to eat.

Since I had two older brothers to run farm machinery and do the heavy outdoor work, I got to spend summer vacation horseback riding and helping Mom in the kitchen. Before I was out of bed in the morning, Mom had sent Dad and the boys off to the field with a breakfast of bacon, over-easy eggs, and toast in their bellies. When I came downstairs, she was ready to discuss dinner plans—always some combination of meat and potatoes—and had pulled packages of home-grown beef out of the deep freeze to thaw.

I remember watching Mom peel potatoes with a sharp butcher knife, shaving a consistent layer of brown away from the white to create a long, thin spiral peeling. She made it look so easy I begged to try. Instead of handing me the butcher knife, she pulled out a potato peeler for me to practice with. Peeling a two-quart saucepan full of potatoes took me forever. My hand got tired and the spuds spent so long out of water the white turned yellow. I whined and begged to give it up. Nevertheless, she encouraged me to keep trying and was always grateful for the help. An hour later, she would rinse my gouged, unevenly peeled specimens and refill the pot with cold water and a pinch of salt before covering the pot and setting it on the back burner.

My next contribution toward dinner was to set the table, fill the glasses with milk or water, and stack slices of white bread on a plate. That finished, I was usually free to go bridle my horse and ride around the yard until the steaks or burgers were almost done. Then it was time to flag the men in from the field. Since we farmed only a half section of ground there on our home place and the house sat on the half-mile point, I didn't have far to go. Mom would step out on the porch with a white dishtowel, and I would ride up to collect it from her.

Buck, my quarter horse, galloped down the road ditch toward the field, my long hair trailing behind me in the wind. I would look for dust blowing up behind an implement. I rode to where the end of the tractor round would be and raised my white flag in the air, the signal that dinner was ready. A wave from the tractor told me I had been spotted. I rode back to the house and helped Mom put steaming, homegrown sweet corn in a serving dish along with the spuds and a platter of meat. The men washed up at the kitchen sink and sat down at the table. After giving thanks, the hungry men made short work of the meal. If a storm was brewing, they would head right back out to the field. If weather was not pushing them, a half-hour nap was the order of the day.

My mother had a hard time catching me to comb the snarls out of my hair. One day after dinner, she took me to Mitchell, where she had made an appointment to alleviate the problem. I went in with snarls and came out with a pixie cut. I remember feeling like a brand new girl—someone I did not even recognize in the mirror!

When we got home from town it was about 3:30 p.m. and time to make lunch. Mom got out the iron meat grinder, fastened it to the countertop, and placed a pan underneath to catch the minced ham when it came out the other end. She fed it big chunks of sliced bologna, hard-boiled eggs, and dill pickles. She let me turn the wooden handle as she stuffed in the ingredients. I was fascinated with the process and thought it was great fun until it came time to disassemble the grinder and wash all the little parts. Mom added salad dressing and spices to the meat and then made sandwiches for the men. She took our old pink infant bathtub off the nail where it hung in the pantry and filled it up with sandwiches cut crossways into points. She covered it with a dishtowel, put in some candy bars, and got a cold pitcher of lemonade out of the refrigerator. We put everything in the backseat of the Rambler Rebel and off we drove toward the hay field.

We slowly bump, bump, bumped out across the hay field to where Dad was bucking up hay piles and lifting them to the top of a haystack with the Farmhand loader. My brother Mark stood way up on top, packing them down with a pitchfork. They happily stopped their hot sweaty jobs for field lunch. Mark jumped into the loader bucket and dad lowered him to the ground. I got out of the car beaming to show them my new bobbed hairstyle. I felt like a princess that day, being the target of both teasing and compliments about my pixie.

As they typically did, the guys stayed out in the field working until almost dusk, stacking alfalfa-grass mix hay. I enjoyed the attention so much at lunch I rode my horse back out for more of it later in the day. I loved the feeling of my short hair bouncing as we galloped along. I loved it even more that night when there were no snarls to tear out with the comb.

As I got older, and after Mark left the farm, my mother entrusted me to deliver field lunch by pony express. I would pack a couple of sandwiches, raisin cookies, and cold cans of pop into canvas saddle bags and ride out to have lunch with my dad. He enjoyed the break, and I welcomed the uninterrupted time with my father. Summer days were long on the farm, working from sun-up to sundown most of the time. We talked about the weather, the crops, a farmer's endless fight against rocks, and noxious weeds.

We discussed how the equipment was running and commiserated about breakdowns. My dad shared memories of farming with horses in the olden days, and in contrast, how much faster things went with modern equipment. I told him about what was going on up at the house, reassuring him I had not forgotten to swing the gate so the feeder cattle could get a drink, and informed him that so-and-so had stopped by to talk about such-and-such.

Pretty soon Dad would stand up, blow his nose in a fresh corner of his red bandana, or just snort into the air downwind, then apply Chapstick to his dry, cracked lips. He would pick up the form-fitting, sweat-stained leather gloves he had plopped on the ground and tug them back on.

"Thanks for lunch, Paula Walla!" he would say with a big grin, crawling back up into the tractor seat.

"Anytime!" I'd smile and wave, urging Buck into a gallop towards home.

Paula Ness Northrup,
Sanborn County

In My Diary From Age Fourteen: Sold!

FEBRUARY 8, 1965

Nice. I put ten dollars in the bank today. The ad for our sale was on the bulletin board.

February 11, 1965

Blizzard. No school this afternoon. Bus brought us home.

February 12, 1965

Cold. Dad stayed home to get ready for the sale. It's going to be a big day.

February 13, 1965

Nice. Men with pickups, loaders, and tractors are swarming around the yard trying to clear away the snow. Dianne, Cheryl, and I had a snowball war with the cousins on the snow pile by the hog house.

February 14, 1965

Nice. We clipped Tiny's other hoof. We brushed the cows' tails to make them look beautiful.

February 15, 1965

The day was bright and clear with a special feeling about it. The chrome on the cars glittered in the sunlight. I followed everybody around all day and I'm so cold. We sold the machinery in the hog yard. I got a hotdog at the lunch wagon. It seems strange to be buying food at my own home. Ray brought four of his pups for us to sell. Cliff bought one for two dollars. I helped Mom this morning and helped Dad last night.

Everyone is proud of the things they bought. Why shouldn't they be? There must have been around 250 people here, at least. Tootsie went around licking hotdog wrappers that people had dropped and Rex drove himself crazy barking at cars. I went in the barn to say goodbye to the cattle before they were sold. Peanuts and another young heifer brought $190 apiece. Tonight we have to milk Daisy by hand. The milkers were all sold. The farm is all lonely and empty. Oh, how I'm going to miss everything so very much.

February 16, 1965

Chilly. I milked Daisy and went to the silo pit to get some silage for her. She is lonesome and moos all the time. Dad helped the rest of the people load the things they had bought.

Linda Gloe Bornitz,
Rural Hartford

Paying the Interest on the Hurley Farm

MY PARENTS, DOROTHY AND EDWARD JACOBSON, purchased the farm northeast of Hurley on November 29, 1950, at a total cost of $14,400 (160 acres at $90 per acre). A down payment of $500 was made that day. The next day a payment of $7,000 was made. Interest of $345 was due on December 1 each year thereafter.

My dad died August 7, 1957. One evening that autumn, August knocked on the door of Dorothy's mobile home on North Main Street in Lennox. Dorothy had never trusted him as Edward had, so she did not invite him in but conversed with him while standing on the porch. The essence of the conversation was that he wanted the balance due on the farm right now. He said, and I remember hearing this, "If you don't pay, I will foreclose on you."

Poor August thought he was dealing with some grieving widow who, out of fear, would cave in. He would have the farm back and would have gained much money on the "deal." He knew not with whom he spoke. Dorothy said, "You will get your interest check by December 1 and that is all I owe you." I am sure she said more, but I do not remember. She stepped inside and slammed the door in his face.

In 1958, when Dick Reiners and his brother-in-law purchased the farm, Dorothy paid August the balance due.

Verlyss V. Jacobson,
Rural Lennox
Printed with Permission from the "Argus Leader" Media

Weed Control

MY DAD TOOK PRIDE in corn and bean fields free of weeds. Since he farmed in the days before chemical weed control, this was not an easy task. The majority of the weeds were uprooted when he went through the fields at intervals with the tractor and cultivator. However, there were always some weeds that grew in the row right with the crop, so cultivating had no effect on them.

Those weeds had to be dealt with. When my siblings and I were old enough to handle a corn knife, Dad called upon us to help him eliminate the cornfield weeds that concerned him the most, the sunflowers and cockleburs. We got up earlier than usual to walk the rows in the fields before the sun was high in the sky and hot.

The weeds in the bean rows were pulled by hand. One summer morning, Mom, Dad, my sister and brother, and I were walking the bean field on what we called "the 80," which was a half mile north of our farm yard. My young brother was new at the task, and he had much to learn. Dad was not pleased when he realized that his son was just pulling a few leaves off the weeds, leaving the roots in the ground.

When we did our weed chopping and pulling correctly, we could all take pride, along with Dad, in the clean fields as the crops matured.

Norma Kruger,
Turner County

The Most Beautiful Crop

MY PARENTS, DOROTHY AND EDWARD JACOBSON, my sister, and I lived on the family farm north of Lennox. In July 1948, Edward came to the house one day asking us to come to the field, where he took pictures. He said it was the best oats crop he had ever seen or probably would ever see. The oats were cut and shocked. My dad hired a transient worker who wandered in one day to help with the shocking.

During that time it rained very heavily to the north. The water moved south in the creek, then spread out over our flat, low land. The water was so deep that the tops of the shocks looked like ducks on a pond. My parents saw it during the night with the moon shining on the water. By morning, the water was receding, taking the bundles of oats along, sweeping them into the creek, and carrying them to the neighbor's property. The most beautiful crop was gone.

Verlyss V. Jacobson,
Rural Lennox
Printed with Permission from "Argus Leader" Media

Threshing

"The threshers are coming," Mom said
As she kneaded loaves of bread.
Water cooled dressed chickens in pans.
She had been up early according to plan.

Out to the garden to pick cucumbers and beans
And other vegetables in between.
My job would be to peel and snap
The produce she brought back.

Dad had harnessed the workhorses in the shed,
And out to the field they were led.
Hitched to hay racks down the lane
To pick up golden bundles of grain.

My uncles came to work the harvest,
All hoping it would be one of the best.
Everyone had a specific job to do,
Making it a fine threshing crew.

The threshing machine looked like a beast
And was about to have a feast.
The men pitched in sheaves of oats,
Swallowed by its mighty, roaring throat.

Separating the grain from straw,
The threshing process held me in awe.
Chaff and dirt flew everywhere.
The men kept working and didn't seem to care.

Then finally it was time to eat.
The men were glad to leave the heat.
They came and washed off some of the grime,
Thankful for the break at lunchtime.

The mounds of dishes were left for me,
While Mom ran to the hen house to see
If the hens had water and gathered the eggs.
Oh, the pots and pans I certainly did dread.

One more lunch to prepare.
We took it to the field with the kitchenware.
More days of threshing were still to be done.
We would have been glad if it ended with just one.

Jan Cerney,
Rural Dixon

Threshing on My Dad's Farm

MY DAD'S FIRST THRESHING RIG was powered by a steam engine that had a steam whistle that was blown as a signal to start threshing at noon, and at night, to quit for the day. Later, he had an Altman Taylor gas engine (It stood 8' to 10' high) that provided the power to make the grain separator thresh the grain. He also had a cook house and bunk house. They were, as you might imagine, enclosed "boxes." The bunk house, or car (they were mounted on steel-wheeled running gear), had bunks two high and usually slept eight to ten men. The bunks, filled with fresh straw, were built-in boxes on opposite walls. The cook car had a division in the middle—half was the kitchen and half had a built-in table on each side, with long benches to sit on. The kitchen had a cook stove, shelves for groceries, and a large table to work on. Staple foods were kept in the cook car, but fresh meat, eggs, and milk were brought in each day.

A lady, hired for the threshing season, did all the cooking, three meals a day, and baked bread, cakes, and pies. The cook car was usually pulled to a farm home where they were threshing, making it safer from fires and easier to fill with water. The plates were enamel pie tins, and the cups were old fashioned tin cups. There was a wash bench at the outside of the cook car, with a pail of water, dipper, lye soap, wash basin, and towels, which hung on nails on the side of the cook car. The men used it to clean up before eating.

Later, the men were fed in the home of the people for whom they were threshing, and the hired men slept in the house. Often, transients would walk in looking for work, supper, and a place to sleep and then would be gone after breakfast the next morning. They often left a present of their "bed bugs." We battled them constantly. Some men were seasonal workers who came every year and were very nice.

Melba Olverson,
Raymond

Spuds

SPUDS ARE THE NECESSARY FOOD for a farm family. They are used in a variety of ways. Fried potatoes grace the bacon and eggs for breakfast. The other meals for the day will either have mashed, boiled, or potato salad varieties as the main dish. It is so important to realize that the potatoes served at the meal take a lot of hard work to put them on the plate at mealtime.

The farm ground is dragged and made ready for seeding. The seed that is used is quite often the yield of the past season that is still in the cellar of the house. There are two main varieties: a red potato and a brown baking potato. Our family raised a lot of the Red River Valley variety.

The day that the planting took place meant going down into the cellar through a trap door at the base of the house. When you went down, it was easy to hit your head. The entrance was not over five feet high. Many times you would bump your head as you went in and out, both in the spring to cut the seed potatoes and in the fall when you refilled the potato bin. The house we lived in had a rock foundation, and rocks lined the cellar sides. We had to use a kerosene lantern to see what we were doing. The potatoes had some good sprouts, and many of them were well ripened and very mushy. It made this an icky job when you had to stick your fingers in them to cut them in halves or fourths to use them for seed. You always had to be sure to leave enough good eyes for the plant growth to sprout in the dirt for the new potato plant. Often a salamander would crawl out of the potatoes just as you grabbed for another one to cut. We put the potato seed on a wagon to fill the potato planter. This planter was purchased on shares with the neighbors across the field.

Around the fourth of July, we would try to steal from the growing potato plant by carefully uncovering some of the produce without hindering the plant growth. Were those new potatoes ever good! The excitement of picking potatoes had pros and cons.

It was hard work, but we were fortunate in having a potato digger that many did not have. It was bought at a farm auction a couple miles from us. With it we no longer had to dig with a spade.

The family liked to have a good fall day for the potato picking. It meant going behind the potato picker and putting potatoes in bushel baskets to be dumped onto the trailer. There were many times during the course of the day when someone was ahead and stooping at just the right angle making it hard not to take an aim at their rear. Then the spuds began to fly. When Dad turned around on the tractor and saw what was going on behind him, it was back to work.

The very last part of the day meant going down into the cellar with the bushels of new potatoes and dumping them in the bin. The cellar was a special place in the life of the farm family where the canned goods, carrots in crocks, and potatoes were stored. I would not trade the good experiences of farm living that I learned with the growing of spuds.

Carol A. Roush,
Hamlin County

ON THE RANCH

SD State Agricultural Heritage Museum Photographic Collection.

Teepee Rings

The Teepee* rings are about all gone,
the ones I've found
just stones,
most no bigger than two fists put together,
all meant to hold a teepee down.
Then, when it was time to go,
with a flip, they got scattered.
Before the Europeans came
habitation was temporary
between the James River and the Missouri.
The old timers talked
of seeing all these stone circles.
I've seen them, too
and did what everyone else did,
which was to throw them
in my tractor scoop
with a thunk!

This I never thought much about
until I climbed some low-lying hills
to the west of my house.
Local rumor was
that Indian graves were on top of these hills.
At the end of my climb all I could see
was a big pile of rocks.
Maybe they were put there by humans,
maybe not.
What I could see was a view
that stretched twenty miles to the east.
A couple of centuries ago,
if I had stood here

I would have seen
buffalo or antelope grazing,
and they would have felt like mine.
The air would have had a breeze up here
nice for a summertime place.
A few feet back from the top of the hill crest
I could disappear from sight
down the other side,
the ridge of a hill
following into another ridge of a hill,
water holes filled from spring melt.
In so many ways
this must have been a good place
to stay from spring through fall.

Someday, in many centuries, will there be
somebody else who will climb this hill and
see a different scene?
Will then they think of me?

Bruce Roseland,
Faulk County

*The Lakota spelling is "tipi."

Dangerous Activities

LIFE ON THE RANCH CAN BE DANGEROUS just by the nature of the business and lifestyle. The rule at our house was, unless there was blood involved, don't scream. If Mom heard screaming, she would come on the run, and if you weren't hurt, you would wish you were by the time she was done scolding (she didn't believe in spanking)!

Lenore had plenty of reason to worry. When her oldest son was three, he took to following his dad, Jack, around. At one point, Jack got frustrated with the little boy's constant questions and being where he shouldn't be. So he told his son to go sit on the mound of dirt a few yards away. Dennis tried to protest, but Jack insisted. He soon figured out his folly when Dennis started jumping up and down and screaming. He had sat on a mound of red ants!

Another time, Jack was mowing. This was back in the days before lawsuits and safety devices. Lenore was taking a much needed break, enjoying a leisurely bath, when the phone rang. Jack went to answer it. Dennis, ever helpful, thought he'd clean Dad's machine while he was gone. He attempted to stick a screwdriver into the blades and ended up cutting off half of his index finger!

Jack's kids made a habit of following him around. Once, his youngest, small for her age, was "helping" Jack feed the cows from the feed bunk. Each summer, Jack would have boys from Sky Ranch For Boys come to help hay and get some experience with ranch/family life that they might not normally get. Well, as Lisa was following her Dad, one of the boys threw a hay bale directly on top of her. Her dad froze. All he could see were her hands and feet; everything else was covered with the bale! Luckily for Lisa, but not so lucky for her mom who had to clean her up later, Lisa had fallen backwards into the forgiving sludge soil tromped down by many cows while they were milling around and eating.

Once, even after being told not to, the Apland kids decided to explore a big truckload of straw that Jack had just purchased but not yet unloaded. As they gleefully launched themselves over the golden stems, one of the kids, Nora Lee, fell into a hole. She was quickly swallowed up, and it took the other two kids—and yes, some screaming—to pull on their sibling's arms, the only things left uncovered by hay.

An event that also sent the Apland kids screaming was the Mad Mom Cow Episode. Dad had to retrieve a dead calf from across the stream. The mother was guarding it faithfully. Dad explained this all to us, and warned that the cow wasn't going to be happy with him, so we needed to stay in the truck. Unhappy was an understatement. That cow chased Dad around and around the truck, pounding her angry head into the driver's side door, warping the door and shaking the truck off two of its tires. Although it probably took very little time and the tires only left the ground by a few inches, to the frightened kids in the truck it was quite an ordeal!

Lisa Wells,
Rural Belle Fourche

Leaving the West River Country

JULY 4th, 1936, WAS ONE OF THE MOST EXCITING EVENTS I can remember. It was time to look for greener pastures. The blizzards and dust storms and the fact that Dad had not harvested a crop in about four years convinced him there must be some better place to go. On this day, Dad hired a big semi-truck to load for moving. It was the biggest truck I had ever seen, even bigger than a threshing machine. Later in my life, I was to spend forty-five years in one. The truck Dad had hired was Glen Trimble's rig with a 30-foot trailer and a new Chevy tractor. We loaded the two workhorses, Nelly and Hoiuche, in the front of the trailer and two cows with them. Next, there were several pieces of farm machinery, tools, and what little furniture we had in the rear. Then came the most exciting part. A couple of light timbers were laid across the top middle of the trailer with a box spring and mattress. Karl and I climbed up and Dad tied us down so we didn't go missing during the night.

Dad, Mom, Sylvia, Katherine, Jimmy, and Fritz, a 4-month-old baby, rode in a Model T Ford coupe. We stopped in Presho, where Dad and Trimble went inside the pool hall to say good-bye and drink some refreshments. We boys stayed tied on top of the semi trailer. A lot of hooting and hollering was going on and fireworks. The horses on our trailer didn't like all that ruckus too well, so they were making a lot of racket too.

After midnight, it was time to go. Karl and I talked almost all the way. We slept a little and awoke just as the sun rose. We never had seen such a sight. In this East River country, everything was lush and green. We noticed that no matter which way one looked at the cornfields, all of the rows, rows, and rows were straight. The mystery wasn't solved until we found out later that it was check planting, done with a knotted wire that was fed through the planter as it was pulled through the field.

We saw Mitchell from our mattress perch—Boy! What a big town! About two hours later, we saw a city that was even bigger. It was something to see, with cars and people everywhere. It was Sioux Falls. We thought that maybe even New York could be that big.

We left Sioux Falls on the last leg of our journey to Uncle Jim Klutman's farm near Rowena, about ten miles out. More excitement came when the Model T showed up, and they told us the car had caught fire back of us only about a mile from where we had refueled. It was put out in time, but could have been serious.

We stayed at Uncle Jim's farm several weeks. I saw his son, our cousin Bernhardt, about two years ago, and he told me then that he had never forgotten what a bedraggled bunch of gypsies we appeared to be. I agreed completely.

We boys stayed at Uncle Jim's farm until just before school started. It was pretty exciting to watch them cultivate all that corn, threshing oats and putting up hay, which was thicker than anything I'd ever seen. One day a train came by and threw some sparks that caught the hay field afire. A lot of neighbors came to fight it. Uncle Jim got overheated and passed out. It was worse than that, I thought, but he came to, and the fire had been put out. Two large stacks of hay were lost.

Robert F. Gloe,
Southern South Dakota
Submitted by Dianne R. Gloe

Biting Off More than I Could Chew

AS WITH EVERY SECOND TUESDAY IN JUNE since I could walk, I was at my uncle's branding in the flat prairies of western South Dakota, just beyond the Slim Buttes. I stood on the palms of my feet, ready to kamikaze myself in front of the escaping calves, should one try to make a run for the gate past the chap-laden men sorting the cows. I was in the seventh grade at the time, old enough to wrestle calves as they were pulled out of the corrals by the ropers, but too young to be responsible for dragging calves out of the pens.

Several people roped the calves and pulled them out. The big boys and girls wrestled calves while the adults branded them, while one or two of the men castrated the bulls, and finally, a few adults gave vaccines, usually with a knee high cowboy following them with marking chalk.

During the first coffee break, one of the kids thought it would be a grand idea to sneak up behind a few of the others and mark up their faces with chalk. This is not your grandmother's chalk. This is mean, unforgiving, oily, and fluorescent scrub-off-until-your-skin-is-raw chalk. I did an excellent job of steering clear of the menacing marking kids, but it did not keep me from manufacturing my own plot for marking one of the older girls. I, unlike these immature kids chasing each other around, was going to wait until we were once again branding to ensure I could put the sneak attack on an unsuspecting beautiful high school girl while she was busy holding down a calf.

Not long after the coffee break had ended and the branding had resumed, I found myself a bright piece of pink chalk lying in my uncle's vet box. I intentionally got to the back of the line of wrestlers to ensure my target would be wrestling before me. Like clockwork, she was the first person to grab a calf as the roper pulled it out of the open. As if I was born to mark this girl's pretty face, I flew in and put a bold, pink stripe across both of her cheeks and quickly ran away. She yelled at me, tried to scold me even, but I could not hear her over everyone's laughing.

The branding continued, and, as I assumed, the pink massacre had occurred without any rebuttal. My glorious thoughts came to a halt as I felt a hand, stronger than my own, reach around and grab me by my forehead as I held down a calf. It was she, and she was gripping my face with a vengeance. What could I do? I had both of my hands on the back leg of a calf as it was being branded, while this older, stronger, girl had a vice grip hand on my face. The surprise increased exponentially as she forced open my mouth and jammed in a raw, freshly castrated calf testicle. I rolled my body over, spitting and gaging, while not loosening my grip on the calf, as I launched the warm, mucous-feeling extremity from my mouth. That was the last time I marked anyone with a piece of chalk.

Michael Anderson,
Harding County

SD State Agricultural Heritage Museum Photographic Collection.

Experiencing Ranch Life

I WAS FINISHED. Finally, four years of college were completed, but I needed to find a job. Like my peers from Augustana College, I attended the Sioux Falls Teacher Job Fair in the spring of my senior year. Much to my surprise, I would soon be hired at Bennett County High School in Martin. My first year was full of ups and downs, but overall I had a wonderful experience and my time was spent experiencing the fullness of ranch life. Let me explain.

As a new teacher I made it known that I wanted to become familiar with all facets of the community and my students' daily lives. Ranching just happened to be a regular part of life out there in Martin, a West River community of about 1,000 people. A couple of my fellow co-workers were wives of local ranchers and invited me to take part in the festivities. By festivities I mean branding season, which occurs in the spring, shortly after calving season.

Branding for a "newb" is a lot of fun, although a lot of hard work is involved. Having grown up in Duluth, Minnesota, I found branding to be a whole new concept. In West River communities, branding is a social event that brings neighbors together and allows kids to earn money. There are two ways to undertake the process of branding. One is by roping and the other is by wrestling. Yes, wrestling is as it sounds and implies. Two people go into a group of calves and grab a calf by one leg each (depending on which side the brand is given). Once the calf is brought into an open area within the corral, it is subdued in order to go through a few procedures. If it is a female, it is branded and sometimes given medication through a pill (given through the ear) or by some other method. However, if it is a bull, it undergoes castration, is given a spray of iodine to heal the wound, given a brand, and sometimes a form of medication. After this horrific process, all calves are let out to pasture to heal and rest up with their mothers. Through the kindness of many families, I have become more South Dakotan by taking part in the ranch life and its duties, which include wrestling calves, branding over 100 head of cattle, rounding cattle up on a 4-wheeler, tagging cattle in the ear, eating the great meal the women made for those involved in branding, and working for the West River Ag. Department in Rapid City by helping graduate students complete their studies over the summer.

In short, the ranch life is bigger than anything I could say or write about, but it is a truly tough life with many perks along the way. I could never have experienced such events without the kindness showed me by the community of Martin. Only through the process of branding does one understand why natives to South Dakota refer to the popular yard game of "ladder golf" as "cowboy golf." This is because when castrating bulls during branding season, their testicles are often thrown and end up sticking or wrapping around the movable metal fencing that are used to make the corrals.

Grant Fifield,
Bennett County

Baling Hay

THE RANCH WAS DAD'S IDEA. He convinced me to apply for the job with the haying crew. He was to operate one of the balers that I would be a stacker for, moving and pushing into place the thousands of seventy-six-pound alfalfa bales generated through the efforts of the irrigators, the swathers, the balers, and the hay sweeps. For a penny a bale. I was thirteen at the time and scrawny. What did I know?

It must have been mid-June when I first went to the ranch with Dad. There'd been rain, and that had slowed down the haying. My first job was out in a field, turning bales so they'd dry on the bottom. I was wearing a pair of high-top western boots, and after I'd turned a couple of bales by kicking them from a side to the bottom and up onto the other side, my boss's second oldest daughter, Janet, called over to me and said that I should be pulling them toward me instead of kicking them away from me. "There might be snakes."

Of course. Rattlesnakes. Crawling under a bale where it would be cool and slightly damp. No more kicking the bales, not even with high-top western boots.

I hate snakes.

Mike, the man operating the other baler, had a snake story one evening at supper. Baling can be a bit monotonous; you make sure you're steering the tractor straight into the swath and make sure the swath is feeding good into the baler. So you look ahead and back, and then you look ahead again. Every once in awhile, you might look around to see where the other baler is and if things are going all right with that one. This is what Mike was doing when he noticed Dad's tractor and baler had stopped. It was not an unusual thing. You might have to check the tension on the baler or unplug the canvas rollers, or something.

Mike said that when he saw Dad, Dad was on his way back to the tractor, a small International. Suddenly Dad jumped, and Mike swore that he could see daylight between the fender on the tractor and Dad's legs. Dad landed with one foot on the seat of the tractor and the other on the footrest. He turned, sat down, and went on with the baling.

There isn't a lot that could make Dad, fifty-three at the time, move like that.

I hate snakes.

One afternoon, Edwin, my boss and the man who ran the hay sweep, dumped off a load of twelve bales on a half-finished stack, and I set about moving them into place. One that I picked up with my hay hooks began buzzing immediately. I didn't even pull the hooks free from the bale. I was just very quickly off the stack.

When Edwin came back with the next load, I told him what had happened. He wasn't satisfied with having a rattle snake in one of his haystacks, so he grabbed the pitchfork off the tractor and we went back to the bale. He didn't think a rattlesnake could live through a journey into and out of a baler, but he wasn't taking any chances. He snipped the twine with his jackknife and began working through the bale with the pitchfork. All he found was a tree locust. Buzzing.

I hate snakes. I hate things that make you think they might be snakes.

For two-and-a-half months I stacked seventy-six-pound hay bales. By the end of the summer, I was no longer scrawny. A penny apiece. $300. 30,000 hay bales.

I'm not particularly fond of hay bales either.

James Cissell,
Meade County

Ranching on the Cheyenne River Sioux Reservation

I WAS BORN AT THE END OF THE DEPRESSION IN 1938 on the Cheyenne Indian Reservation. Times were getting better during the late 1930s. The reservation has a land base of over a million acres of rolling hills and prairie grass, which is high in protein. The reservation was controlled by the BIA and a superintendent on the reservation. The tribe leased the reservation lands to the DZ Cattle Company until the railroad closed down, then they leased them to a horse company called CBC Company owned by the Chaplin Brothers from Chicago. After the drought, the CBC Company pulled out and gave the horses that survived the drought to tribal members.

The tribe started a cattle program called the Repayment In-Kind Program, which gave cattle to tribal members. The idea was to get the tribal members to become cattle ranchers. No money was involved with this program. Prior to 1934, every Cheyenne River Sioux Tribal member received 160 acres of land, called allotment land. The rest of the land was controlled by the

BIA area office in Aberdeen.

I raised Hereford beef cattle on my parents' ranch, and it became my ranch after they passed on. The land was comprised of trust land, leased land, and owned land. In my twenties, I was a saddle bronc rider in rodeos when I wasn't helping raise cattle on the ranch.

After I had heart surgery in 1988, I had to discontinue ranching and the rodeo business altogether. My sons continue to raise bucking horses and presently have approximately 250 head of horses on the old CBC ranch headquarters in White Horse, now known as the Gunville Ranch.

Harlan Gunville, Sr.,
Cheyenne River Sioux Indian Reservation

Roadhouse Memories

I WAS BORN IN A ROADHOUSE in the inland town of Edson, ten miles south of Faith on the future Highway 212, on January 20, 1915. Growing up in a roadhouse was different from a regular ranch. It was similar in some ways to present bed and breakfast establishments, except that our guests rode horseback and brought their cattle with them. They were trailing the cattle to the nearest railroad, the Chicago, Milwaukee, St. Paul, Pacific, (CMSTP) in Faith. The cattle were held in pens until they could be loaded on the train for the Chicago Stockyards and market. Owners were given a free pass to ride in the caboose, so they could see that the cattle were unloaded at various points for food and water to avoid their losing weight before they were sold. Dad went with the cattle to Chicago to visit his good friend Mr. Mosher, a fellow homesteader who as many adventurous Easterners had, found he was better suited for city life.

The Sederstrom roadhouse was a composite of abandoned homestead shacks which had been moved on skids pulled by horses. Mother served the cowboys their supper and breakfast. Dad fed the horses and put them in the smaller barn, with stalls and a hayloft, for the night. The cattle were kept in a fenced pasture, so the men did not need to stay with them. The pasture was not used by our cattle so as to provide grazing for the visitors and to prevent our stock from the threat of anthrax.

The cowboys had trailed cattle from as far as twenty to thirty miles; they had traveled about ten miles a day, so they were ready to sleep in one of our bunkhouses, each of which had two beds. They slept two to a bed and used the outdoor toilet. To wash up in the morning, they came to the house, where Mother had a teakettle of hot water for them to use in the enamel wash pan.

In the fall, the ranch owners came with their wagons to get supplies for the winter. Since we were just ten miles from the end of the railroad at Faith, they stayed overnight with us, rose early in the morning, and came back to our place to stay another night before returning to their ranches near Edson, Bixby, Fox Ridge, Opal, or Sulfur. These little places had stores and a post office and were called "Inland towns" because they had no railroad.

Helen Sederstrom Barney, Deceased
Edson

ANIMALS

SD State Agricultural Heritage Museum Photographic Collection.

Farm Pets

EVERY FARM KID KNOWS THE DIFFERENCE between a work animal and a pet. That didn't stop my siblings and me from trying to make pets out of most of the animals on the farm where we grew up. Often, it didn't work!

I had a special fondness for baby chicks. I could not resist those little cheeping balls of fluff. I was fascinated by the brooder house full of their tiny black eyes in a sea of yellow. When Mama sent me to feed the chicks, I would wait until they were comfortable with me standing in their midst. Then, I would clap loudly—once— to see all those black dot eyes go down at the same time as the chicks reacted to the unexpected sound. I do not think Mama would have approved, but I thought it was great fun.

As a rule, chickens do not make good pets, but I remember a particularly friendly little rooster we named Oogie. We could get him to perch on our shoulders or follow us about. I suspect he grew up into one of those mean roosters that loved to chase me.

Of course, we had plenty of cats. Those that survived the annual bouts of distemper made great pets, as well as keeping the farm's rodent population under control. We loved dressing kittens in doll clothes, but we had a terrible time trying to get them to stay in the doll buggy. Even Mama had her favorite cats, a tiger-striped gray and a solid black. They whiled away many a cold winter day snoozing under the cook stove in the kitchen.

Dad usually kept a couple of dogs on the farm. He trained them to herd the cows home from the pasture at milking time. Each dog had its special place in our affections. I can still remember most of their names—Sport, Beauty, Spike—and Dad's special favorite, a huge black and brown dog he called Maddo. They were good pets and loyal friends.

Occasionally, we'd tame a bucket-fed calf or befriend a little runt piglet that needed to spend a few days in a box beside the stove in order to survive. They were pets only while they were small. We kept our distance from Daddy's big workhorses, Dolly and Bill.

Eventually, we did have one animal that was just a pet. That fat little black pony named Bertie had no practical use whatsoever. The only way we could get a ride on her was to push, pull, or somehow lure her up near the house. Then one of us would quickly jump onto her back and hang on as she galloped back to the barn, where she preferred to spend her days eating and sleeping.

Many of my happiest childhood memories involve the hours of contentment spent playing with pets. I learned much from them about love and responsibility. But they also taught me the importance of just having fun.

Marilyn Kratz,
Bon Homme County

Farming With Horses

GROWING UP IN THE 1920s AND 30s on our farm near Mission Hill was a good time. We farmed with horses, primarily, though Dad owned a Sampson tractor, a very temperamental piece of equipment which we used for grinding feed for livestock. The harnesses for the horses were stored in a corner of the horse barn when not in use. They were draped over a number of pegs and hooks when not being carried around on the backs of our four-legged friends.

Part of our chores was preparing the horses for work in the mornings and getting them unharnessed and out of the barn at night. Starting at 5:30 and 6:30 a.m., we would place a measure of grain, usually an oats and barley or corn mixture, in the feed box located in the front of each stall, open the barn door, and let the horses into the barn, being careful not to get trampled in the process. The older and more mature always went to the same stall and were secured with a halter while they were eating. Sometimes, the younger ones would go to the wrong stall, creating extra work for the horse handler, as he would have to back them out and get them to their proper stall and haltered. This could be difficult, as his partner would notice the full feedbox with no one eating from it, which proved too much of a temptation. He would help himself to a free lunch, incurring the wrath of the horse handler and the disappointment of his stall partner. Working horses required a certain amount of grain to keep up their strength, so an extra portion would have to be doled out. Handling these 1200 to 1800 pound animals was no job for the timid. It was an excellent time to get your feet stepped on or get squeezed against the wall or between two of the sometimes contrary beasts.

Depending on the fieldwork load, we had from two to fourteen horses to get ready for work, and during harvest time even more, depending on whether the neighbors took their horses home at night or not. A certain amount of skill was necessary to manipulate the reins in order to make turns at the end of the field without tipping equipment or tangling harnesses, horses, or equipment in such a manner as to be dangerous to both driver and horses as well as threaten to break machinery. Drivers spoke to their teams a lot, either to direct, encourage, or calm them, or sometimes to berate them.

Barn cleaning, a never-ending task, was a dirty job. Horses have a sizable amount of ammonia in their urine, and when the barn had been closed for any length of time, due to winter storms or whatever, the stench would make your eyes water. You could always tell when you needed a half-sole job on your shoes when you felt the juice squeezing up between your toes as you walked into the stall and stepped into a wet pile of horse dung.

In those days, we had traveling horse traders moving through the country in their wagons, driving a team and herding a number of horses of various descriptions behind them. We usually had extra horses to trade, and I remember one time Dad traded one of our less desirable work horses for a beautiful saddle pony.

William R. Cutts, Sr.,
Rural Mission Hill

Thousand Pounders

WHEN WE WERE MARRIED IN 1946, my husband and I started our farming venture with a cow and calf, two sows, and twelve hens given to us by my husband's parents. By the early 1950s, we had more than enough milk for our own use, so, for storage, we purchased a bulk tank. The milk was then picked up by a milk truck and sold to a dairy.

When my husband saw the ad of a nearby neighbor who was selling good milking Holstein cows, we decided we needed another cow or two to fill that bulk tank He went to look and brought a couple of them home. The farmer said they would calve soon, but he thought they could be milked for a week or two before the calves were born.

I helped with the milking and we were not using milkers yet, so I milked by hand into a bucket. One morning, one of those new cows lifted her foot and brushed me off the milk stool, dumping the milk all over the barn floor. I told my husband about it, and the next milking he watched her do the very same thing. He decided to leave her out of the milk barn until the calf was born. About a week later he came in the house fuming. "I'd like to see the bull that fella used on his cows. Her calf is so small it can't even reach the cow's teats!" he complained. "I milked out some colostrum so you can feed the calf with a bottle."

Later I went out to check on the cow and saw that she was lying down. I expected her to be up by the barn bawling for her calf, but she was not interested. As I got closer, I saw another small calf lying by her side. When she stood up, there lay a third calf behind her!

Triplets! No wonder that first one was so small. I named them Eenie, Meenie, and Meinie. But there was no Moe. Two were bull calves and one was a heifer. Now I had three calves to feed on the bottle, which was quite a chore. We got a couple more milk pails with nipples, since we had one already. Then each calf had a pail.

Since they were Holsteins, the calves grew fast and soon were turned out into the feedlot with other feeder calves. Usually the bulls get larger, but little Meinie grew just as fast as Eenie and Meenie. One year later, the fattened triplets went to market weighing a thousand pounds each. Mama Holstein turned out to be an exceptional milk producer after all. But after the triplets, she never raised more than one calf at a time.

Berthetta Ness,
Sanborn County

145

Racing Horses at Bear Creek

THE HOME WE KIDS WERE RAISED IN was originally a log cabin built in 1906 by my Grandpa's uncles on Aunt Cecelia's allotment. We called it Bear Creek. It is situated on the north side of Bear In the Lodge Creek just before it turns north to eventually empty into the White River.

When we were young, my brother, Kent, and I spent many summer days riding our horses. They were old and gentle. His horse was Buck, a tall, big-boned buckskin gelding that Uncle Jim used to ride. Buck's lasting legacy is a comical combination of actions that kept Kent on guard. The sequence would begin with Buck throwing his head downward and coughing, followed almost immediately by a loud fart, the sound of which startled him, causing him to jerk his head up and to bolt forward. At that moment, Kent had to quickly reel in the slackened reins or else tumble off Buck's hind end.

Spot was my horse. She was a fat paint that Aunt Jo used to ride.

Those horses tolerated us. We did not know their youthful accomplishments as ranch horses. Since we rode without saddles and were too small to swing atop them, we devised all manner of ways to remount when away from a fence or deep trail. They patiently stood as we pulled on their tails and manes, shinnied up their legs, swung from their necks, and used their hocks as ladder steps. They seemed indifferent to us, and being so much bigger and stronger than us, they sometimes got headstrong and paid little heed to our kicks or tugs on the reins, especially when we were headed toward home. But one afternoon on our way home Buck saved my life.

It happened while the four of us were racing homeward in the draw northwest of the house. Spot and I had taken the lead, she at an all-out run and I with my legs pulled up like a jockey. Buck with Kent atop was running as fast as he could, thundering along just a couple lengths directly behind us. Something startled Spot, and in that split second she shied and I lost my balance and fell to the ground. As I rolled, I caught a glimpse of Kent tugging at the reins, pulling Buck's head up and away. But they were too close and running too fast. I stopped rolling on my back, just as Buck was upon me. And as I lay there, a huge hoof came to rest inches above my chest. He held it there, seemingly unaffected by Kent pulling for all he was worth on the reins, and I shimmied out from underneath it.

Even though that happened over forty years ago, I believe I could still point to the exact spot where I lay, anticipating the bone-crushing weight of Buck's left front leg pressing into my heaving chest. Spot circled back and the four of us proceeded home, never saying a word to anyone about the incident.

Craig Howe,
Martin

By Jean Laughton, Used with permission by
Jean Laughton.

Mustangs

WE WALKED OUR HORSES SLOWLY OVER THE LAST RIDGE, hoping we wouldn't scare the mustangs. Daddy and I were checking the water tank for the third time that week. It had been a hot dry summer and the creek had dried up. The only water in the south pasture was from the windmill.

Daddy was riding Fancy, the tallest horse on the ranch. He was a sorrel with four white stockings. However, that wasn't why they called him Fancy. He had a beautiful, high-stepping prance that made him look like he belonged in the king's parade, so someone named him Fancy.

I was on Shorty, the oldest, fattest, slowest horse on the whole ranch. But at least I was out riding, not at the house, playing paper dolls! The first thing we saw as we topped the rise of sand hills was the windmill turning gently in the breeze. It was easy to count the turns because one blade had broken in a strong wind and it looked like a big pie in the sky from which someone had snitched a half piece.

Then we saw them. They stood together, head to tail, fighting the flies for each other in the shade of the big cottonwood trees. You could hear a foot stomp occasionally, and a snort drifted our direction on the breeze. Good! That meant the wind was blowing our scent away from them and we might sneak closer for a better look.

Daddy and I sat quietly for a while, just watching. The colts were all up beside their mothers. They had just finished watering and hadn't gotten a chance to lie down for a nap. The big sorrel stallion was closest to the tank. He was the one that would spot us first, but he was swishing flies, taking a break from guarding the herd. He was facing into the wind and lifted his nose, flaring his nostrils once in a while, just to make sure no strange scent came in on the breeze.

"Can you get a count, Charlie?" We always counted the mustangs. If some were missing, we'd have to look for them. "This is a good looking bunch of colts, don't you think?" He wasn't really asking my opinion. He was stating a fact. He loved those mustangs.

We turned our horses and walked them slowly back over the sand hills toward home. "Shorty is getting old and slow, Charlie. When we bring the mustangs back to headquarters next week, you can have your pick," Daddy said, talking around the stem of bluegrass he held between his teeth. I knew just which one I'd pick. She was a Paint, white with brown spots so beautiful they turned bronze in the sun. I named her Patches.

Patches and I became best friends. We explored the ranch together, sometimes going her pace, and sometimes mine. We knew the day the pheasant eggs hatched in the stack yard. We watched the spring start flowing in the Badlands. I stayed in the saddle to pick plum blossoms along the creek in the spring and then picked ripe plums in the fall. I rode her bareback to the one-room school and then she ran home alone.

The joy of riding one's horse on South Dakota's prairie is about as close to paradise as you can get.

Claudia Little,
Rural Kadoka

Turkeys and a Tail Wind

DAD AND MOM RAISED ABOUT 150 head of turkeys during the dust storm years to try and bring in extra money to take the place of crop failures. Raising turkeys took help from all of us. Feed was a minor problem, as grasshoppers were so thick that it made up nearly the whole diet of the birds. We butchered them to make it to the holiday markets. All the turkeys had to be plucked clean and the insides taken out except for the gizzard, heart, and liver, which we put back inside. The necks and feet were packed enclosed in brown paper bags, and the turkeys were then packed into wooden barrels for shipment to Peter Fox and Sons in Chicago. Dad would put the barrels on a wagon and bring them to Presho. They brought a nice check just in time for Christmas.

There was not that much work in raising the turkeys, except for two separate times when they took off from home. It seems that a hard tail wind would start them, and they didn't know when to stop. Both times they ended up at the Henry Bowers ranch up by Stony Butte, about five miles north of our place. The first time they went up there, after we found out where they were, we went on foot and walked them all the way back home. They were real easy to herd, but it made for a long day. Then the turkeys took off again, the same bunch, but this time they were herded home with Carl and me on horseback. We sort of enjoyed that. That was the end of that bunch of roving turkeys' wandering days, as their next trip was on the train to Peter Fox and Sons.

Robert F. Gloe,
Lyman County
Submitted By Dianne R. Gloe

Cracked Eggs

THE NUMBER OF CRACKED EGGS MOM HAD on hand often dictated our family menu. Fried, scrambled, poached, or cooked eggs were common for both breakfast and supper, and what better way to use a dozen eggs than in angel food cake? Since the angel food used only the egg whites, Mom made a jelly roll from a recipe that called for a dozen egg yolks.

During my growing up years in the 1940s and 1950s, Mom, like most farm wives, did the chicken chores. Chickens were raised, not merely to provide food for the family, but the selling of eggs provided money for those groceries which could not be grown on the farm. Mom gathered the eggs from the nests in the chicken coop in the late afternoon each day. She placed them in a wire basket, and in the prime laying season, she came from the chicken coop with eggs stacked in two baskets.

She carried the eggs into the basement of the house, where she washed them. Collapsible dividers of light cardboard were opened and placed in the bottom of each side of the partition in a heavy brown cardboard crate. A clean egg without any cracks was placed in each small compartment of the dividers. A flat cardboard was placed on top of each tier of eggs. Layer after layer was added on each side until the crate was full. The cracked eggs were put in a separate container for home use. Sometimes the crates of eggs were taken to a grocery store in town to be sold, and other times a buyer of eggs had the truck route to pick up the crates from area farmers.

When Mom visited with farm neighbors and friends, the price of eggs and the current egg production of their hens were discussed. The young hens, known as pullets, produced small eggs, and even though they tasted just as good, their size affected the price received for them. No longer having pullet eggs in your basket was good news to be shared with others.

Mom entrusted me with the gathering of eggs when I was big enough to carry the basket. On one occasion she was not happy with the large number of cracked eggs I brought to the house. After that I never forgot that the egg basket was not to be swung back and forth as I carried it from the chicken coop to the house. No doubt the eggs were on the supper menu that evening.

Norma Kruger,
Turner County

A Hereford Heifer for Christmas

MY HUSBAND AND I WERE MARRIED just three short months when Christmas 2004 was rapidly coming upon us. Being of a practical nature, George was not going to buy frivolous items. Soon he had come up with an idea about what to give his newly-wed bride. He had heard his wife tell him many times that her Daddy, a Hoosier farmer, believed that Hereford cattle were the only ones to have in the herd. He thought, "It won't be so bad to have a lone Hereford in a Black Angus commercial herd!" So on Christmas Eve he asked, "Suz, would you like a Hereford heifer for Christmas?" I gave a resounding "Yes" and was thinking my late father would be so proud. Then he made a hasty call to a respected Hereford breeder in the neighboring county, and a deal was made over the phone. By making this deal, George proved he was a true knight attired in rugged ranch wear who was willing to do anything for his lady-love ranch wife. He had agreed to trade his two best Black Angus replacement heifers for one Hereford heifer!

Next, the old blue Ford was hitched to the stock trailer and down the road we went to view a nice assortment of Hereford heifers. I even got the privilege of choosing my Hereford heifer. My husband unloaded his Black Angus heifers, loaded my dark, red-hided beauty christened Stella, and we headed for home.

Along the way, George said, "I don't know what the neighbors are going to say about this Hereford." I replied, "Oh, the fellows may get a chuckle or two but not for long because their wives will be asking, "Why didn't I ever get a pet cow of my own!"'

Suzanne England,
White River

The Circling Steers

WHEN I WAS SEVEN, many things that had never bothered me started to scare me. The bulls in the pasture across from our house were mean. Cars could crash into other cars. My older brother might fall from the ladder on the roof of the barn while he was shingling. In the winter, when a hundred head of cattle came in from the pastures and stomped around the feedlot in the farmyard, the beady eyes of corn-fed steers gave me nightmares.

The following winter, at the mature age of eight, I finally admitted the fear I had of the monsters in the nearby feedlot. One particular steer-filled nightmare prompted me to crawl into bed with mom and dad at three in the morning.

The next night, after he had fed the cows in the feedlot and we'd already eaten supper, Dad told me to put on my boots, snow pants, and coat. He took my mitten-covered hand in his and we walked across the darkened farmyard.

I didn't want to go into the feedlot, but Dad insisted. Once we'd passed through the electric gate in the fence, the light from the yard-light by the machine shop cast a white glow on the steers in the far corner. I turned toward home, but Dad whispered, "We are going to stay here until they form a circle. I bet you didn't know that cattle will form a circle around you if you wait long enough."

I grew curious at that, and I felt safer with Dad at my side. I had seen a cow go after Mom before. Dad, however, controlled animals; they didn't control him.

We stood in the middle of that feedlot. I held Dad's hand extra tight. Slowly, the steers began to walk toward us, their moist noses frosting the air as they exhaled. One by one, the steers went into formation, forming a circle around us, as Dad had said they would. They stepped closer and closer together until the circle was closed up, and every creature in the feedlot was eyeing us in curiosity.

"If we wait here long enough," Dad whispered, "They will come right up to us and sniff our arms. Do you want to wait here even longer? Or, are you getting too cold?"

My teeth chattered, as I whispered back, "I want to wait."

One steer stepped closer, bridging the gap from ten feet to five feet. Then another followed, and soon they all had tightened the circle. From that distance, their eyes didn't look mean, but curious, as their heads lifted and sniffed the air, detecting our scent. They were so close the heat from their bodies made the cold air grow noticeably warmer

Dad asked, "Do you get it yet?"

"Huh-uh, get what?" I replied.

"They are more afraid of you then you are of them," he assured me. As Dad spoke, the ear of a steer perked up, and the animal took a step back.

"Get! Go on!" Dad suddenly yelled. The steers broke the circle apart, running to the opposite end of the feedlot in a panic.

And then I got it. Dad taught me a great truth that night. The scary things in the world that stomp and glare, cause nightmares and needless worry, and seem full of evil are actually just as scared of me as I am of them.

Andrea Beyers,
Rural Bowdle

The Petrified Pony

PETRIFIED WOOD IS, AND PROBABLY WILL ALWAYS BE, a hot commodity in landscapes surrounding houses in the Midwest as well as across the nation. I was living on a ranch in the northwest corner of South Dakota. It was not unusual for us to ride horseback anywhere from four to eight hours in a day moving, doctoring, pairing, separating, or simply checking cattle. As I would trot across the grassy flats, I would try to pay close attention to the ground around me, not necessarily watching for hazards, as the horses were usually in tune to their hooves' landing pads, but on the lookout for other peculiarities. Often, I would find antlers or skeletons from antelope or deer, or entire skulls of longhorn cattle. Excitement occurred when I would discover a piece of petrified wood.

It was the hind end of a long day, and my cousin and I were on our way back to the barn when I saw a piece of petrified wood poking out of the sand near the river that split the ranch. As I expected, this rock was a small piece connected to a much larger piece buried underground, much too deep to pull out on my own. I made a mental picture of the area and decided that I would come back to find it with a fresh horse the following day.

The next day, I saddled a horse named Turbo. Turbo had a brain of his own. The only problem was his brain was pretty well scattered. He was the kind of horse that would squirt or jump at everything, and he was chargier than most world champion steer wrestling horses, but he was one of my favorites. Armed with an old ranch rope, Turbo and I set out to find my piece of petrified wood. For the entirety of the ride to the rock, Turbo kept looking back towards the barn, obviously waiting for one or two of his friends to join us, as it was unusual for us to be alone. Turbo's dizzy headedness began to rise exponentially as the barn disappeared out of sight, and he began to realize that we were going on this adventure solo. I could see the stress in the whites of his eyes as we finally came to the end of our jog at the petrified rock.

Never one to plan, I was not sure how I was going to remove the rock from the sandy bank of the Grand River, but I tossed my rope around the rock and dallied it up around my saddle horn. I did not need to kick Turbo to encourage him to go; I simply turned his head toward the barn, and he lunged up the small bank, clearly unaware that we were going to be pulling out a rock. Turbo was caught by surprise as the rope pulled tight, so he tried to jump away from the rope. Simultaneously, I saw the rock pop out of the sand as I was launched off of the horse into a somersaulting heap in the sand. Angry and embarrassed, I pulled myself together, picked up my thirty-pound, thousand-year-old rock of shame and started walking home as Turbo sprinted back to the barn. I left the rock next to the gravel road, not far from where I found my reins. Turbo had snapped them both off in his escape. Luckily, he did not get hung up. I finally made it back to the barn to find Turbo who had found himself into an open corral, about twenty feet away from my cousin, who was sitting with a smug grin on her face as she held her disposable camera, ready to take a picture of Turbo, the saddled, reinless, rock-pulling horse, as his rider walked red-faced through the gate.

Michael Anderson,
Harding County

The Runaway

FATHER AND I WERE ON BEN HASSELAAR'S PLACE driving a wagon, filled with fencing tools, and being pulled by a team of horses. I was somewhere between four and eight years old. I was "tending" horse—actually I held the lines as the horses stood and nibbled growth on the stubble. "We" were checking fence on the south side, preparatory to putting cattle on the stubble. This was often done in summer following threshing. Ben H. had no cattle. He, a city farmer, ran the threshing rig; so we sometimes used/rented his stubble fields in the 30s. As we worked our way slowly to the east, Father would verbally direct the horses to go a ways and then command them to stop. I would assist by pulling on the reins. However, this time, instead of stopping, the team bolted—taking off to the east. I pulled for all my might. Father ran after the wagon hollering, all to no avail. One of the horses had rubbed his bridle off, making control harder. The team rounded the corner at the east end and went north. When they got to the driveway, they kept right on going through the ditch. The box flew off the running gear—I with it—and it landed upside down. I was thrown clear into a bit of mud (it had rained). Finally the horses stopped—total runaway distance was about one-half mile—and father caught up with them. He got the wheels back to the box, lifted it back onto the running gear, and put the tools in again. Then, before he had me come on again, he gave those horses "Sam hill" up and down the road: "If you want exercise I'll give you some." Exciting memories to a boy. As I write this, tears come to my eyes.

Chester VanderZee,
Douglas County

Pet Skunk

ONE SUMMER SATURDAY EVENING AROUND 6 P.M., as the family was leaving for church, we spotted about three baby skunks in the ditch along the road. I was about twelve years old at the time and had always wanted a pet skunk.

I told my Dad to stop the car and he pulled over to the side of the road. Thinking the skunks were too young to have developed scent sacs, I decided to catch one. In the process, I was sprayed, but I continued after them anyway! I managed to catch one but was not allowed into the van with the skunk. We went back home and got a live-coon trap to put it in.

The family then headed on to church, but I smelled so bad from the skunk that I had to sit in the car during the service.

The next Monday morning, Dad and I talked to the vet at the sale barn in Gettysburg and to Doc Nold about de-scenting the skunk. No one would do it, so that was the end of my pet skunk.

Nathan Nagel,
Rural Gettysburg

Learning About Hogs

IT WASN'T UNTIL I GOT MARRIED AND MOVED to a hog farm that I realized that adult hogs were bigger than I was! Soon after that I realized they were nearly as smart as I was too!

Growing up in a very small western South Dakota town, I was well aware of the importance of agriculture, although my limited expertise was with cattle and wheat rather than hogs and corn. But in the blithe manner of the twenty something crowd, when my husband suggested moving to Lyman County and raising hogs, I went along with it. My education about the porcine psyche started with a crash (that would have been the sow breaking the feeble gate to the farrowing barn) and continued apace.

Over the next eight years I learned a few things.

First and foremost, no matter how closely you calculate the due date on a sow, she will always litter in the furthest corner of the open lot the day before you move her into the barn. Moving a sow with twelve piglets squealing at the highest pitch audible to mankind is not an easy job. Every sow on the place will respond to the piglet distress cries, and fences are not an obstacle.

The intelligence of a sow with piglets is amazing. Forget the fact that she may lie on one or two, she still counts them. Snout to piglet, she snuffles down the line. If one is flat, she noses it out of the way and apparently subtracts it from her total.

Gardens with watermelons, tomatoes, and other fresh veggies are immensely attractive to swine. Our garden was a delectable draw to the resident hogs. In fact, I have seen pigs push at one end of the swing gate on their pen and when it didn't open, trot to the other end, shove their snout under the gate, and lift it off the pegs, which allowed it to swing freely, thus allowing them to amble across the yard and indulge in what I had planned to can for the coming winter. And pigs are picky. If the first bite of a melon wasn't ripe, they just left it and checked the next!

In a similar vein, if you ever are carrying buckets of feed for free range pigs, never, ever, stop your forward progress. They will immediately surround you and the buckets will be emptied then and there!

Orphaned piglets are a whole other story. They are loveable, smart, and pretty fun to have around the house. Garbanzo joined the household because he was the runt of a sow who had farrowed fifteen piglets and had "faucets" for fewer than that. He was a red Durroc and smart as could be. He drank from a bottle and was content with his box and heat lamp until he discovered he could escape the box and come down the hall and into the bedroom demanding food. He was easily trained to use a litter box and then had free run of the house. Since he was an "inside pig," he didn't have the obnoxious hog smell, and the click of his hooves heralded his arrival in any room.

Farrow to finish operations are not the same today as when I met my first adult hog. I'm quite sure that piglets born in twenty-five degree weather don't end up on the oven door to warm up, and quite probably the farrowing barn is nicer than the mobile home we lived in more than thirty years ago.

Improvements in barns and hog raising not withstanding, I'm very glad I'm not a nursemaid in a farrowing barn any more!

Micaela E. Nelson,
Rural Kennebec

Piglets in My Kitchen

SHIVERING IN AN EARLY MORNING of the cold winter, I hugged my robe tighter over flannel pajamas. A storm had begun the day before, New Year's Day 1949. Our toddler son was still sleeping, cuddled in bed with his dad for warmth. We lived with my dad on his family-owned ranch, south of Hot Springs, on the Cheyenne River. He had suggested we move there when my husband was released from World War II military service the year before. We were anxious to begin our new life and left the east coast for South Dakota.

As I reached for a chunk of wood to stoke the kitchen stove on this snowy day that began the notoriously severe blizzard of '49, devastating the Dakotas and surrounding areas, I heard my dad, "Pop," stomping onto the back porch. In a gust of wind-blown snow he entered the kitchen, carrying something in a blanket.

"Quick, bring a blanket," he directed, as he lifted three frosted little pigs from the basket. While he was doing morning chores, he saw them fall through the ice-crusted river, rescued them, and hurried them into the house. We wrapped their cold, still, little bodies in the blanket and placed them on a bench in

161

front of the open oven door. As we anxiously watched for signs of life, their round, pink, little bodies warmed and began to wiggle. All three were alive and ready for action! Midst a furor of squeals and grunts, their pink snouts began to root about in search for mama pig and sustenance. We lowered them to the floor while we found a covered box to house the squealing piglets, and Pop transported them to the barn and the comfort of mama and her dinner buckets.

Living conditions at the old ranch were primitive, but we were determined to handle the challenge. There was no electricity or indoor plumbing. Kerosene lamps provided light, and an outside toilet was down a path from the house. Doing the laundry was an immense task. We resurrected an ancient, hand-operated washer. It required considerable arm strength to swish a paddle back and forth to agitate the clothing through the sudsy water. Water for the process was drawn up from a well by a bucket on a rope, then carried into the house to heat in a boiler on the kitchen stove. I did the almost daily baby laundry on a scrub board. To dry, the wet items were carried outside to hang on a clothesline. Of course, they froze to the line in winter, which actually whitened and made them purer and softer. Ironing and pressing garments were done with "sad irons," which were heated on the stove. Danger of scorching was a constant threat. Our baby's bottles of formula were kept cool by lowering them into the well. Later, we learned to cut large chunks of ice from the frozen river, then store them in a shed of sawdust. An icebox in the house was kept filled with the ice for food preservation.

The ranch house was about two miles off the main highway, accessed by a dirt road which crossed the Cheyenne River. There was no bridge across the river. Most of the time the river could be driven through, but there were times of increased water flow, or flooding, which prohibited crossing by car. The usual alternative was to park the car and wade to the other side, rolling up pant legs or tucking up skirts as high as possible. Sometimes, husband waded through ice-crusted water, arriving at the house extremely chilled and shaking (probably causing his crippling arthritis in later years).

Though living on the ranch was a primitive lifestyle and involved a lot of hard work, I loved the still, quiet atmosphere and fresh air with the wafting fragrance of the river. Even the sound of distant yipping coyotes was soothing.

Naida R. McKinney,
Rural Hot Springs

How the Man Broke Horses

He rode the familiar plain toward
Swiftwater, dark and seething, murderous
in the heat and dust of a hundred years
of Dakota hunters outwitting their luckless prey. The sleek
blooded roan beneath him needed fire, foamed wet
at the mouth from chomping at the bit, prancing witness
to a day's hard night. Not even a wedge of light
from ravines and side roads shadowed the hold
angry gods had on him.

From the other men's wives he slept with
while mastering moonscape and prairie wilds
not a dime's worth of thanks
for his lust. His beauty was a tribute

to this ancient tribe, pipedream now
from the lonely and triumphant cannibals.

Ovation was not his thing, no need for
applause, no Orphic devotion to the oldest principles.
The civic-minded better step out of the way.
When he was young he loved Big Pipe's place
and spoke the names of those
who knew what it was like
to ride a horse down. Reverently.

Elizabeth Cook-Lynn,
Crow Creek Sioux Reservation

By Adrienne DeBoer, Used with permission by
Adrienne DeBoer.

BARNS AND
BARNYARDS

Photo courtesy of the State Archives of the South Dakota State Historical Society.

Tales From the Great Red Barn

WE KIDS LOVED OUR GREAT RED BARN. It was our fun hideout. When the cousins came to visit, we headed for the big hayloft to swing on the hay ropes and drop into the loose hay that was stored there. Another favorite game was "Hide and Seek." My sisters and I knew every inch of the place from the silo room to the feed bin, which enabled us to hide from the cousins.

Other adventures included hunting for a new batch of kittens and tracking down the nests of our wily Bantam hens. Many afternoons were spent exploring all regions of the barn. Mother always knew where we were and what we were doing— most of the time. At least she knew that we were within calling distance.

The main floor of the barn housed the calf pens, cow stanchions, and horse stalls. We trained our 4-H calves by enticing them into the stanchions with some ground feed. After clicking them into the wooden stanchions, we would lean out of the adjoining stanchions and brush and comb our calves. In this manner we tamed our own calves, and by the time dad was ready to help us teach the calves to lead, they were easy to handle. We didn't need any hard hats or other safety gear. The stanchion was our safety zone.

As I reflect on the inner workings of the great red barn, one humorous adventure comes to mind. The horse stalls had been constructed for large draft horses. After dad sold the workhorses, he kept the stalls for tying up bulls and heifers. One of the horse stalls was smaller and just the perfect size for a single pony. My younger sister Marie and I both loved this stall, and naturally we fought over who got to use it. Another advantage of the small stall was that it was closest to the big barn door for easy access. Often we raced our steeds into the barn to claim the first stall. On one hot summer day after riding my horse,

Hi-Fi, I came to tie him up and brush him down. Marie had not ridden her horse that afternoon, so I knew that I could use the first stall. When I came to lead my horse into the stall, there painted in bright yellow letters was a sign on the stall with the words, "Marie's Pony—don't touch!" The paint was still wet, so I had to take Hi-Fi to the second stall. I was rather miffed as I walked to the house to find the culprit. I found her hiding behind Mother. To make a long story short, Marie won the battle. Mother reasoned that since Marie's pony was smaller than my quarter horse, her pony should have the smaller stall. I really didn't appreciate this turn of events, and, to this day, I still think that I heard my mom laughing about my younger sister's unique sign. (In retrospect, it was a pretty good sign for an eight-year-old.)

Barns are supposedly just structures—they don't breathe, talk, or have feelings. But, in the case of the great red barns or white barns of the prairies, most owners would tell you a different story. These proud owners would relate that their barn was a living, breathing, feeling monarch who had held court over their farm. May our landowners continue to pay refurbishing tribute to these invaluable heritage monuments.

Jane Green,
Watertown

Hero of the Grain Bin

BENJAMIN WAS TEN, ALAIN WAS SIX, and the kittens were three weeks old. Lester was taking apart the old grain bin during combining. He was not pleased and really wanted to be out in the field. Anyone who drove into the yard would be very confused to see him doing carpentry repairs at harvest time. But Alain had taken two baby kittens, climbed up to the second floor of the bin, and dropped them between the walls. They were trapped.

Benjamin had witnessed it all and was sure they needed to be saved but hadn't a clue how it was to be done, so he was yelling, and crying to us—us being Leonid, the Russian hired hand, and me. We were stuck in the mud with a tractor and a wagonload of wheat by the auger at the west barn.

After Lester got in and fixed that problem, he took a look at the old grain bin. We were able to open up an inside panel by the outlet and free one kitten, but the other was between the outer walls on the south side. We had to take off the outside wall panels and the inner panels, trying to get to the second kitten, but we couldn't see it.

Lester sent Benjamin to get a flashlight. After twenty minutes, I went to the farmhouse to check on him. Ben decided that the flashlights wouldn't work because they were dirty, so he took the biggest one apart and was washing the batteries in the kitchen sink, while crying for the poor kitten. The corroding was already underway when I grabbed him and the plug-in electric light by the door and headed back to the grain bin, where Lester had located the kitten by sound. We found it without more trouble.

Benjamin was thrilled to see the second kitten safe and saved.

"Daddy, you're a hero!" he exclaimed. He was obviously very perceptive. And his persistence saved two kittens, although the flashlights and batteries were ruined.

Later that day, Alain asked us, "If I'd fallen between the walls, would you have tried to save me?"

While I hugged and assured him that we'd always take care of him, Lester asked, "Would you be holding kittens at the time?"

Rosemary Dunn Moeller,
Hand County

Haymow

EVERY YEAR THE HAYMOW WAS STACKED HIGH with rectangular bundles of prairie hay. An old yellow rusted corn elevator transported the bales from the sled below through the narrow opening into the mow. Pigeons roosted on the large hemp rope running lengthwise along the crest of the barn. This rope kept the large, never-lowered door in place and was tied off on a wooden ladder nailed into the north end of the haymow.

Several generations of chickens laid and hatched their eggs in this mow. Momma cats hid their kittens in the labyrinth of hay and preyed on wayward chicks that wandered from their clutches.

The matriarch of the farm gathered eggs from the haymow and used them to make cookies, cakes, and delicious pastries. In the morning, she'd scramble or fry up a couple dozen of them, and at Easter she'd boil and festively color them with food dye.

In the summer of 1974, two brothers, nine and seventeen, were given the paid task of cleaning the haymow while their parents went to town. The parents harbored some hidden doubts as to how well they would perform the task, but the brothers wanted the money and the haymow desperately needed cleaning.

An Allis Chalmers D-17 tractor with hayrack attached sat parked in front of the majestic barn. Each young man wielded a four-pronged pitchfork. The temperature outside was in the upper 90's, quite cool compared to the muggy haymow.

The brothers worked hard, making a game of it. Several rotten eggs were found under the successive layers of yearly chaff and hay which littered the floor of the mow. Many of these eggs may have predated the youngest brother, and when downward pressure was applied from the mass of a person stepping on top of them, they exploded like mines in a minefield, popping and emitting sulfuric gas into the already stuffy atmosphere. The brothers kept tally of the mines each other stepped on. A certain number of detonated mines meant a kill for the other. The object was to be the one killed the least often.

The hours rolled by as the old hay and straw were forked out the narrow door exiting the haymow. The rack below filled with ages of discarded hay, straw and eggs shells of exploded sulfur bombs. Sweat, dust, and chaff clung to the brothers' backs, and their hair was matted to their heads.

The task was completed with nary a straw to be found on the wooden floor of the haymow. Both brothers, sweat drenched and tuckered, smiled with pride as their parents inspected the immaculate haymow.

Daniel G. Snethen,
Tripp County

Windmills in the Dark

MOST FARMS HAVE WINDMILLS. I believe our grandparents intentionally and strategically placed them in dark, remote locations on a farm knowing they could scare the "bajeebers" out of their youngn's who were called upon to turn the windmill off on dark nights.

Upon returning home from visiting friends or relatives, I dreaded hearing "go turn off the windmill" from my Dad. But one just did it because you were not about to tell him you were too scared to do so. On our farm between Lake Norden and Bryant, the windmill was located behind a grain shed and the barn . . . in the dark. To turn the windmill off, one pulled down a wooden stick and slid a hooped wire up around the stick to stop the windmill from pumping water. Otherwise, there would be a huge mud puddle around the tank. It was fine to a 10-year-old boy to turn the pump off in the daylight, but another story to do so in the dark. I bravely walked to the back of the barn, saying to myself, "There ain't noooo boogie men around here, no sir"! I got to the windmill and pulled down the stick, lifted the wire, and calmly walked under the "X" cross members supporting the structure. As soon as I was clear of the mill, I took off as fast as my short, fat legs could carry me. If the Olympic trials for the hundred-meter dash were held between that dark windmill and the safety of the lighted house, I would have been in, hands down. Only the Lord could have caught me, but he would have had to have been in his best condition!

There are far more great "non-scared" memories of being raised on a farm, but I wonder how many others might have had this same experience.

Dewayne Kangas,
Rural Bryant

Baling Wire

WE'RE TOLD WE LIVE IN A WIRED WORLD. I think they used the wrong wire. They should have used baling wire, because the computer certainly isn't solving the world's problems. Baling wire once held everything in its proper place, but you don't see much of it anymore. Maybe that's why the world seems to be spinning in the wrong direction. Baling wire had a thousand uses after it had served its intended duty embracing a bale of hay.

Our old 1936 Chrysler, with a hood as big as a helicopter pad, was literally held together with baling wire. Shelves in the garage hung from baling wire. When a buckle broke on a four-buckle overshoe, baling wire was called to serve. It also held the black, round stovepipe in place in our living room.

Our screen door hook was fashioned from a twisted loop of baling wire, and a hole in the screen had been patched—sort of—with baling wire. The heat lamp in the chicken house swung from lengths of baling wire wound around a rafter. A bent hook of baling wire held a plump, upside-down rooster while the feathers fell before Sunday dinner. The wooden-handled windmill brake was imprisoned in the "off" position in a loop of baling wire wrapped around the mill leg. The long-handled tin cup for drinks from the well swung from a hook of baling wire.

One of the rites of manhood was for a boy to be asked to get out of the wagon or car and open the wire fence gate. It was held in place by loops of baling wire at the top and bottom of the support post. The trick was to push your weight against the gatepost that was held in those baling wire loops and flip the wire loop up over the top gatepost. Opening the gate was the fairly easy part. But closing it sure separated the men from the boys.

Seven decades ago when we drove in our rattletrap, baling-wired Model T to Uncle Ed's farm, my dad would go on a baling wire hunt after dinner before we left for home. He worried that a day might come when we'd run out of baling wire so necessary to meet the little emergencies back in town. It was needed to wire the rain gauge to the fence post, repair the broken garden rake handle, hang a new set of license plates on the car's front bumper, snug firm the brake arm on my old second-hand bike, or hold mom's tall hollyhocks in an upstanding position out on the sunny side of the house.

In the 1930s, baling wire kept the world's wheels from wobbling. If only today's problems were so easily rectified.

Chuck Cecil,
Brookings

Our Windmill

OUR FAMILY MOVED TO A SMALL ACREAGE about ten years ago, and I began to wish that I had a windmill. My husband and I noticed several on our way to and from work, usually at abandoned farmsteads. The windmill and surrounding trees were sometimes all that remained to indicate someone had lived there at one time. Usually the windmills had parts missing. Sometimes only the tower remained. The blades or the tail were missing on others. We talked about calling the owners to see if anyone would be interested in selling, but the logistics of taking apart and moving a forty- or fifty-foot-tall windmill seemed formidable.

I'm not sure why having a windmill on our rural property was important to me. My uncles had a windmill on their farm, and I still remember the rhythmic, clanking sound that the pump made as it worked to bring cold water to the surface from the well below. I also enjoyed seeing the scattered windmills that provide water for the rangeland cattle in the desolate Nebraska Sand Hills. Maybe I'm partly fascinated by windmills because they seem to belong to a vanishing farm landscape, like the old wooden barns that used to take a community to build and now slowly crumble and disappear.

One spring day, I went out to the workshop and discovered that my husband, Jim, was building a windmill for me for Mother's Day. He was able to hide the project when he was making the blades and tail, but the tower was too large to stash away when he wasn't working on it. He and my sons had cut the blades out of sheet metal, welded them on to a circular frame and balanced the blades by gently spinning them. When it appeared heavier on one side, they attached wheel weights to the ring on the opposite side until it spun freely. My husband also cut a tail out of sheet metal and welded it to the shaft holding the fan blades, then welded together eight-foot lengths of angle iron and cross braces to make a tower. With a finishing coat of silver paint, the windmill looked like it was made out of galvanized metal.

At first, I thought it would be fun to put the windmill to the south of the house, down by the garden fence but realized that we didn't have many windows that face toward the garden. We placed it to the east of the house so we could see it during all of the seasons of the year. Now, I watch our windmill from the kitchen window as I make coffee in the morning and through the glass door at supper-time. We check it throughout the day to see what direction the wind is from and how hard it is blowing. When the weather is stormy, sometimes the fan swings back and forth or spins around in a complete circle. There is something soothing and reassuring about watching a windmill, sort of like watching a campfire. The wind is always changing, sometimes stronger, sometimes weaker, sometimes switching direction or stopping altogether.

Maybe the fascination lies in being able to see a force that is usually invisible to us.

Last April, we came home after a trip to find the windmill mangled. Apparently a blade had broken off during the strong spring south winds, and the nearby blades had gotten twisted and bent. I searched a wide semi-circle to the north of the windmill, but couldn't find the missing blade. We hated seeing the disfigured windmill every time we looked out of the window, so Jim took off the fan to repair in the shop. While he worked on it I noticed that the tail of the windmill was still working, telling us which way the wind blows.

Ruby Wilson,
Brookings County

Special Places

MY CHILDHOOD ON THE FARM was a mostly solitary existence. Sure, there were brothers and sisters and cousins, but relatives are the friends you can't choose. The tradeoff was discovering all of the places I could go with myself.

Most of those places were up—up in the hayloft, up on roofs, up inside grain bins. I'd climb the steep cobwebbed stairs to the great open expanse of the haymow, then climb the risers of bales. The hay, stacked on the south side, was easier, the rough bricks of alfalfa clenching each other like burrs.

The straw bales on the north end were smoother and slicker, shimmering in a way that made me think that Rumplestilskin's work was half done before he began. But straw bales also were treacherous, having a way of leaning against each other so that they sometimes silently slipped into a small avalanche. The roar always came afterwards, when Dad discovered the tumble.

Sometimes I would hear him from the roof of the milking house, which was the best place to get away because no one ever looked on roofs for a kid. I'd first slip into the small office of the milking parlor to filch chocolate chip cookies from my aunt's deepfreeze, then tuck them into the waistband of my shorts so I could climb the iron rings that hugged the silo, up onto the roof.

From that vantage point I could see into Minnesota, even Iowa, or pretty close. I wonder now what I thought during those long afternoons—besides hoping that my aunt never noticed the missing cookies. I know that I daydreamed whole dramas with myself as the heroine, victim, savior, or star. Such rampant self-esteem was the great privilege of being alone.

Yet there always were lots of people on the farm. My uncle's family lived in a house north of the shelterbelt, and the hired men almost always came with wives and kids. So I couldn't have been so much alone, which tells me a little of how memory works. Maybe this recollection of the solitary farm life is more nostalgia than fact.

But then I remember the day that I climbed up the straw bales, so late in the summer that they reached almost to the very rafters, I remember jostling each before I stepped fully, trying to gauge how well they were nestled.

They were high enough to reach an unexplored angle where a grain bin took up a corner of the loft, no longer used now that we had steel bins in the south yard. A ladder was nailed to one wall, and I eased myself over the lip of the bin and onto the rungs.

The bin was cool, the thick timbers so necessary for strength also keeping the heat at bay. I descended into the dim depths to discover that the ladder only went part way. I realized that if I fell, there was no good way out except to yell until someone heard me, which would have been a very bad way out.

So I climbed back up, frustrated by the end to my adventure. Only later did it become clear to me that had I fallen, had I been knocked unconscious or even died (see victim daydreams, above), no one might have found me for hours, even days. It simply wasn't a place anyone would check. That's how alone I was. And there still are days when I wonder how I might have figured out a way down to the granary floor, where no one would ever look.

Kim Ode,
Brandon

HOME

SD State Agricultural Heritage Museum Photographic Collection.

Around the Kitchen Table

As a FARMWIFE, one of the things that sets me apart from my counterparts in town is the amount of cooking I do. Fortunately for me, and all those who gather at my table, I enjoy cooking. We don't exactly live out in the boonies, but we're still twenty some miles from the nearest McDonald's. When you live miles from a nearby restaurant, you learn to cook. Home cooking not only saves money, but it saves my guys precious time from commuting to and from the nearest eating establishment.

However, I know that our mealtime is more than nourishment. It is a time when my husband, our two grown sons, a brother-in-law who travels from town, and other paid employees who have become "family members" gather around my kitchen table. As a farmwife, I consider it very important to host daily business luncheons over the noon hour. Now my clientele do not wear three-piece suits, not even leisure suits. It's "casual Friday" every day here. Instead of Wall Street Armani duds, they sport denim jeans and layer shirts that may have seen their better day, with hooded sweatshirts displaying seed corn or livestock pharmaceutical logos. Don't let their attire fool you. They are definitely businessmen, and business is definitely discussed. What's been done and what needs to be done is the general table topic. They sometimes even discuss what the neighbors have done and what they need to be doing. Markets, or the lack of them, often come up in the conversation. A lot of letters are thrown around: FSA, USDA, CCC. DENR, NRCS, SDCA, NCBA—well U C—don't U?

Any way you look at it, the infamous family farm table is as central and credible as any small business office furnishing. I don't appreciate phone calls in that time period or having to go to town to take in a noon meeting, because, frankly, I'm busy from 11 a.m. to 1 p.m. Meal preparations and clean-up time generally take longer than two hours. My guys are hungry when they come in, and a mere cold-cut sandwich doesn't cut it. We still have pretty traditional meals here. That means a variety of "meat and potatoes" or "potatoes and meat." Aw, sometimes the guys will go out on the taste bud limb and venture into ethnic foods like stroganoff, enchiladas, and pizza, but none of that fusion cuisine that I get in my Bon Appetite magazine. Actually, my guys are not fussy eaters. They eat their veggies and follow the unwritten clean plate rule. When I fuss about what to feed the guys, my husband reassures me with, "Don't worry about it. If they don't like it, they can bring their own lunch in a brown paper bag." I haven't seen one yet.

Karla Pazour,
Rural Pukwana

The Big Iron Cook Stove in the Kitchen

IT'S SO EASY TO FEEL WARM AND COZY these days as the winter winds blow around our well-insulated houses. All we have to do is move a tiny dial on the thermostat and we're as warm as we want to be. Perhaps we'd be a bit more thankful for that "instant warmth" if we thought for a few moments about the days when the source of heat in our homes came partly from our own exertions and never did reach the corners of the rooms.

The farm house in which I grew up had two sources of heat—the big iron stove in the kitchen and a kerosene burner in the dining room. Heat from the kitchen stove wafted up through a register in the ceiling to warm the bedroom over the kitchen where we children slept. The kerosene burner in the dining room wasn't used unless we were expecting company, so I'm sure our parents' bedroom over the dining room was often downright cold during the long winter nights. No wonder we all used down-filled mattresses and covered ourselves with thick woolen blankets.

Many of the best memories of my childhood home center on the iron cook stove sitting at one side of the big square farmhouse kitchen. Mama kept its pale green enameled sides and black cook top spotless and gleaming. The reservoir on one end had become rusty, so we didn't use it to heat water for cooking, but there was always water in it. Attached to the top of the metal sheet extending upward from the back of the cook top was a warming shelf, the perfect place for storing crackers to keep them crisp. It also held a pile of hot pads and the large green glass salt and pepper shakers with their dented tin tops.

We burned dry corn cobs in the stove most of the time, and keeping the cob box filled was a job for us children. Every day after school, out we'd go, bundled up in flannel shawls over our heads, warm coats, and heavy gloves. After we'd filled the galvanized tub to the top, we'd stick in a row of cobs upright around the rim so we could add another four or five inches of cobs. By the time we were done, we'd be a bit warmer already.

Warmth radiated out from the cook stove, doing a pretty good job of heating the entire kitchen, but it was always warmest right next to it. Sometimes, in the morning before the stove could even begin to warm the kitchen, Mama would allow us to open the oven door and lean on it to get warmed up after coming in from milking the cows.

I can still smell the soups simmering at the back of the stove on cold winter days and Mama's fried chicken, which needed to be cooked near the front of the stove where the fire made the surface the hottest. But nothing ever tasted as good as a slice of Mama's homemade bread, toasted directly over the hot coals in the firebox. No modern toaster can even come close to that flavor.

Mama and Daddy eventually added a three-burner

kerosene stove in the kitchen. After we got electricity, an electric stove and gas furnace in the basement replaced the old iron stove. But whether it was bathing on Saturday nights with the tub sitting right beside the stove or pulling the kitchen table a little closer to it to play board games, those wonderful times of a family cozily interacting in a kitchen heated by a big old stove still warm my memories.

Marilyn Kratz,
Bon Homme County

The Slop Pail Shuffle

THE DARK, DANK AREA beneath our sink, in the days of my youth near Wessington Springs, was where we hid the slop pail and the other devious tools of the kitchen clean-up trade. It was home of the U-shaped rag—petrified with age—resting serenely in the crook of the sink drainpipe. There was also a rusting can of silver polish there that was always a mystery to me because we didn't have silver. We had stainless steel utensils, including a few forks with missing teeth.

We also had a ponderous pig that owed its existence to the contents of that rusty old slop pail occupying a place of honor under our sink. Emptying that blasted slop pail was a difficult chore for which none of us kids ever vied. We tried to ignore its festering, fermenting mass until it was full to the brim and maybe even losing a bit that slithered down the pail's wooden handle.

The slop pail held everything imaginable, from eggshells and coffee grounds to pancake rinds, orange peelings, apple cores, grandpa's used-up chewing tobacco, and other accoutrements that might accumulate at the table and stove. There was probably even a tincture or two of soapy water in the slop pail and maybe the final sliver of a bar of hand soap that had calved, slipped its moorings topside, and tumbled silently into the pail. It wasn't a pretty sight—the slop pail—except to our pig rubbing nervously against the homemade hog trough on the high ground in the makeshift pen, waiting for his handout.

Once that slop pail was at overload, it was time to feed the hog. Getting the pail to the hog was my job. I detested the thought of carrying the heavy, heaving slop pail that looked as if it could explode at any minute. It required some fancy footwork for a stumpy-legged kid like me. We called it the slop pail shuffle.

I carried the pail two-handed, swinging it back and forth between my legs with my nose held high to avoid the aroma, making sure that the mass remained at peace with gravity so some of the contents wouldn't break free. The swinging also helped take the pressure off a spindly arm for a few nanoseconds of that long walk to the pig trough.

Of course, some of the slop pail's contents always did find freedom, mostly taking refuge on my pant legs and in my pant cuffs. On the day I carried the slop pail, I could pretty well plan on eating my school lunch alone.

But the pig loved the contents of that slop pail. It grew and prospered, and after it was gone to market, we'd get another one to handle the kitchen overflow. And I would continue to perfect the jerky dance known as the slop pail shuffle.

Chuck Cecil,
Brookings

Early Refrigeration

WHEN WE LIVED ON THE FARM north of Lennox, we had no electricity prior to the summer of 1948. A barrel of water by the well, which was near the barn, was our refrigerator.

Water coming from a well is very cold. The water from the well first went into a 50-gallon barrel. A pipe from the well entered the barrel about six inches from the top. Another pipe exited the barrel on the other side and carried the water from the barrel into the tank from which the cattle drank. Cold water dropped to the bottom of the barrel, thus keeping a relatively constant cool temperature.

Milk, butter, and leftover foods were put in glass jars, which could be capped to be air and watertight. The jars were dropped into the barrel. Heavy items sank. Lighter items, as a jar partially filled with mashed potatoes, would float. When mealtime came, someone had to leave the house, walk to the well (my memory says it could have been a block away), get the food items, and bring them to the house. I remember leaning over the barrel and reaching to the bottom to get jars. It is a wonder we didn't fall in and drown. After the meal, the items had to be returned to the barrel.

Electricity arrived in 1948. Ah, refrigerators and lights. No more smoky, smelly, kerosene lamps.

Verlyss V. Jacobson,
Rural Lennox
Printed with Permission from the "Argus Leader" Media

The Boxcar House

SOMETIMES I LIKE TO SAY THAT WHEN I WAS A CHILD I lived for a few years in a boxcar. In fact, I did, although it was attached to a small house on a farm. This was my father's ingenious solution to enlarging a house when he needed to move his family to his farm and didn't have much money. In the Depression of the 1930s, my father lost his job as postmaster in Newell and had to find another way to make a living. Years before, he had homesteaded some land a few miles from town and was developing a small dairy, although he didn't intend to live there. We had a cozy little house in town. A hired man lived in the two-room house on the farm that was built as part of "proving up" the homestead. Dad built a big barn with concrete floors and stanchions for twenty-four cows. There was a milk house where milk was pasteurized and separated and bottles were sterilized. It had hot and cold running water and a walk-in refrigerator. These were the important and necessary facilities for a Grade A dairy. However, there was just that small, two-room house with no such amenities. Now he had to bring his family of five to live there.

Railroads were an important part of South Dakota's landscape in the 1930s, and surplus boxcars were available for various uses. Some of these were brought to farms to house migrant workers who came from Mexico to work in the sugar beet fields. So my father thought, why not? He bought a boxcar and had it transported to the farm and cut in half. The two halves were attached to the south side of the tiny house, one on the east end and the other on the west end. In between these two parallel wings he built a sort of entryway or porch. The westernmost boxcar was converted to a small office and a bedroom for my sister and me. The eastern side became the kitchen. My parents had the sole real bedroom, and my brother slept on a daybed in the living room.

Windows were cut in the ends and sides of the boxcar additions. On the west side, at least, they had awnings. Wall covering was "butcher's paper," which was pink and sturdy and nailed to the wall with lath. We had an outhouse and a washtub filled with water heated on the stove for our Saturday night baths. Eventually, Dad added a small shower to the milk house so we could occasionally use that.

I was too young to realize how poor we were and how hard my parents worked to deliver milk to customers in town at three cents a quart. With contracts to provide milk for the cavalry post at Fort Meade and the CCC Camps at Orman Dam and Camp Crook, my father made a go of the dairy for a while. When I was seven or eight years old, I thought it was a wonderful place to live, with cows, birds, dogs, cats, chickens, wild roses, big cottonwood trees, and, of course, an endless supply of milk. But drought and debt overcame the operation at last.

We left the farm in 1940. There were more hard years, but nothing like living in a boxcar at the farm. In the end, my parents prospered. The last time I drove by the old farm I saw that the magnificent barn had fallen down and was a pile of sticks. I was sorry to see that.

Lorraine Collins,
Butte County

Strange Music in the Air

DURING THE LATE 1960s, an ordinary farm family was settling in for the evening. They paused for their supper meal of the usual meat, mashed potatoes, and gravy, with maybe a side of vegetables. WNAX was the daily weather and music station playing the airwaves.

Behold! Another sound was interfering with the frequency. A stirring. A thump. A hardy plunk. Was that erratic beat coming from the radio, wondered the missus, or could it be from the basement? The hole in the ground below the kitchen was not really a basement, but merely a dugout. Crumbly plaster somewhat covered the dirt walls, while the floor itself was dirt. Just plain dirt. This cavern housed the dilapidated cupboard securing canned fruits and vegetables and an old electric hot-water heater.

Since farmer husband was ravenously feeding himself, the missus took it upon herself to tramp to the back entry, pry open the trap door, and peer down into the blackness. Could that be my quart jars swimming toward the wooden steps? she gasped. Then the missus screamed.

As the farmer husband entered the scene to survey the situation, the missus bellowed, "How deep is the cavernous lake?"

"It's nothing much," he threw back, as he began to pull on hisfive buckles to plod down the steps.

"You can't step into those muddy waters," pleaded the missus. "You could get electrocuted down there."

"Who else would go down there?" he gruffed. "There'll be a flood if I don't."

The water heater had sprung a leak. It was propped off the soil atop several stacked-up cement blocks. According to the husband, there was no need to worry about getting electrocuted. Good grief! The water had not crept up that high yet. There was no rowboat in sight nor would one fit within the walls of that cellar. So in he waded, pushing jars aside as he would fish in a lake.

Job done. Water turned off.

Jars were laboriously rescued from the hidden lake the next day. A long-handled broom snagged the applesauce, peaches, and beans. Some were dug up from the miry clay after the water dried up.

The food was canned, wasn't it? Can't hurt to use them. All that work can't go down the drain. Wash off the jars and they'll be fine.

All through the winter months the farm family was fed from the canned goods, and so were some invited guests who came to the table. Little did they know that the jars were salvaged from the muddy waters of the cellar.

Now wouldn't that make a fine title for a song on the air? "Salvaged Cellar Jars." It has a strange twist to it!

Doreen Ronning,
Rural Nora

DIVERSIONS

SD State Agricultural Heritage Museum Photographic Collection.

Fun and Games on the Ranch

ONE OF THE PERKS OF RANCH LIFE is that you have access to a gigantic natural playground. There are acres and acres to explore, boulders for innumerable jungle gyms, and ponds and streams to wade in. Forts can be created in unseen gullies, battles fought on slopes and fields, and thoughts can be put together without interruption.

Jack and Lenore Apland loved to have fun with their kids, friends, neighbors, and large extended family. It was understood that most Saturday nights or Sunday afternoons would be spent in the company of at least one carload of guests. Lenore made a habit of baking a cake on Saturday morning to serve people who came to play cards that night. While the kids played "King on the Mountain" or "Kill the Carrier," the adults might join in for a game of softball, "hide and seek," or kick ball. Once, during a game of hide and seek, the Apland kids nervously told their mom that they had "lost" dad. After an intense search, Jack was found—on the upper branches of a tree—with only the "cherry" of his cigarette giving him away.

Chicken would be cooked in anticipation of Sunday after-church visitors. People loved bringing their kids to our big playground to run around, hunt, play cards or games, or just sit around the big kitchen table and talk.

Then there were the traditional events. Christmas was a time when Lenore was left to her own devices—baking wonderful smelling treats, while Jack took the kids up to the west pasture to hunt for their tree. Although he already had the tree picked out, he would unload the kids near the site, then let them wander, slowly herding them towards "his" tree. The ranch house had tall ceilings that allowed wonderfully tall, long-needled pines to liven up the living room. On New Year's Day, an all day celebration was held, not only to ring in the New Year, but also to celebrate his daughter Nora Lee's birthday. Lenore would entertain the others, while Jack, all of the kids, and some of the braver adults would brave the cold to build a bonfire near a wide area on the frozen creek. Then they would all ice skate through the afternoon.

Lisa Wells,
Rural Belle Fourche

Amusing Ourselves During Threshing Runs

THOUGH WE WORKED VERY HARD during threshing season on our farm near Mission Hill, there was a lot of fun and camaraderie. Sometimes, as we pulled our wagons of bundles into line, awaiting our turn to unload, we would sit in the shade of the hayrack, playing mumbly peg, swapping stories, complaining of the heat or the cold, and indulging in all kinds of horseplay. I loved to instigate it.

One prank was to run a post through the rear wheels of a rack. When the driver tried to pull his load up to the machine, the wheels would not turn. The horses could not pull forward, so the driver would have to climb down off the load to determine the problem. This in itself took quite an effort, much to the merriment of his buddies, who would be hiding behind some of the machinery, acting as innocent as babes.

Another trick we enjoyed doing was to remove the steel pin from the doubletree hookup to the wagon and replace it with a wooden peg. When the team started forward, the pin would break, and the horses would lunge away from the wagon, expecting to be pulling a full load. This, of course, could pull the driver off the load if he happened to have too firm a grip on the lines. We always pulled this on one of the younger guys, because the fall from eight or ten feet high was one you didn't expect an older person to be able to take. Surprisingly enough, no one was ever badly injured when this trick was pulled. These pranks always resulted in considerable cursing, along with very sincere vows of vengeance against the culprit who initiated the prank, and just to make sure the victim got the right one, he would work on us all, again perpetuating the pranks.

William R. Cutts, Sr.,
Rural Mission Hill

Rural Electrification, Television, and
Charlie Starkweather

DWIGHT EISENHOWER WAS THE FIRST PRESIDENT I remember. But a promise made by Franklin Delano Roosevelt in 1935 to get electricity to all American farms made FDR the first president to affect my life in a major way. In the autumn of 1955, as a third grader, I watched the installation of the "highlines" for their march into the hills (the Coteau des Prairie) from State Highway 25 (now 27) up to Hillhead, at the end of the county road past our farm. The reality of World War II had stalled FDR's Rural Electrification Project well beyond his ten-year projection. Finally, we would have electricity with its promise of timesaving devices and extended hours of productivity. Mostly, I was waiting for a television. My father and several uncles cut a hole into the side of our small house to fit in the most compact television from the Downie Jewelry and Repair shop in Britton. It took three men to lift it into its eye-level alcove.

By January 1958, when my story takes place, we were used to being modern. When anyone was awake and in the house, the television was on. News of the world came through the NBC affiliate in Fargo, North Dakota. Reception was always a little grainy, but a trip outside to turn the pipe wrench permanently attached to the antenna mast might help. "Is it better?" Dad would yell into the house. No. Turn it a little more," Mom would holler back. When the TV image jumped and fluttered and defied recognition, we knew it was the "damn Northern Lights" again. But the television stayed on. My favorite shows were the "Ed Sullivan Show" with its plate jugglers, "Playhouse 90" with live dramatic plays, and once, wonder of wonders, Mary Martin flying across the screen as "Peter Pan."

Television also carried news from around the world. January 1958 brought horrible news from too close. Two juvenile delinquents from Nebraska—Charlie Starkweather, 19, and his dungaree-clad girlfriend, Caril Ann Fugate, 14—were on the run, having already shot and killed three members of her family. In all, eleven people were shot or stabbed, often just to get a car. The newscaster did not know where they were headed—maybe Canada.

The highway past our farm led straight into North Dakota and then Canada. On the map, Nebraska was nearly straight south of us. The locks on our doors were flimsy and never used anyway.

"They won't come this way. Don't worry," my Mother said as I sat at the kitchen table and looked out the dark window. Through the bare branches of our shelter belt I watched the car lights heading north.

At our one-room schoolhouse the next day, also located on a section road just off the highway, we were alarmed by the sound of a John Deere tractor outside. It was Jimmie Semple's grandfather, Giles, already out spreading manure on his field across the road from the school.

"Is everything okay?" he shouted over the loud machine.

"Yes," my Mother, the school teacher, waved back.

Giles, a veteran of World War II, pointed to the American flag hanging from its pole. It was upside down, a universal call for help. But it was just a mistake made by the boy who had hung it in a hurry that morning.

Later that day Starkweather and Fugate were caught. The news said there was a high-speed chase and a gun fight outside of Douglas, Wyoming. A map of South Dakota was found in one of their cars.

Angela Ilene (Gunderson) Henriksen,
Marshall County

West River Farmers, the Radio, and Other Big City Habits

I GREW UP DURING THE THIRTIES in Brookings, where we had electricity, indoor plumbing, mechanical refrigeration, and a radio. My mother had cousins, maybe nineteen or twenty years old, named Bennie and Henry Weiss, who lived and worked on their family's farm near the tiny town of Orient. Once they visited us and were completely captured by our modern amenities, especially our radio. They were so glued to the radio that my mother could hardly pry them away from it, even for meals. I recall that my dad liked to listen to "Amos and Andy," and he was greatly disgusted because Bennie and Henry had the radio monopolized when it was time for his program.

We once visited the Weiss farm and went with them into Orient for church on Sunday. I'll never forget how the Weiss boys went to the tavern for a beer and a smoke after church. They also kept some beer cooling in their stock tank. These facts shocked me, a kid nine years old, since drinking and smoking were completely alien to the beliefs and lifestyles of my farmer-uncles near Brookings. I thought that farmers did not participate in these citified activities.

Denton E. Morrison,
Orient

The Rotten Eggs

MY FAMILY'S LIFE has always been full of treasured and unexpected moments. One of these involved the rotten eggs.

Our farm was located a few miles away from our home, and we would drive over in the morning to do chicken, duck, and turkey chores. But the story actually begins when my sister and I helped nurse two wobbly turkeys to full adulthood. After all, turkeys are frail younglings. Well, when both hen turkeys, named Curious and Dunes, were fully grown, they decided to settle down and raise a family or start a nest.

Shortly before the natural urge to start these nests struck the two hens, a tom turkey was added to the barn yard. His name was Duke. Everyone was expecting baby turkeys in the spring.

Spring came about quickly, and Dunes was the first turkey to start a nest. She finally had a full nest of at least a dozen eggs. On a nice hot and sunny day, we drove over to do chores. We were running a bit late that morning, for my sister had to get to work. She diligently ran over to where Dunes was sitting. She admired the eggs and ever so carefully lifted one out from under Dunes.

"I think we have baby turkeys!" she exclaimed.

"What do you mean?" I inquired curiously, stepping a little closer.

"Well, if you shake the egg lightly, you will hear a small thumping noise, that's the baby turkey."

"If you hear a thumping noise, it's probably rotten," Mom warned, walking over to us and taking the egg from Jacinta, examining it incredulously.

"They're not rotten," Jacinta protested, only to jump as Mom abruptly tossed the egg to the ground, as if she knew she only had seconds before something explosive would happen. She was right.

What followed was deadly. It felt as though all eyes watched the egg topple through the air in slow motion. The bomb was threatening us all, and there was no turning back. Poof! Splat! A mix of gray and green substance exploded into the air as it hit a nearby chicken perch, exploding upon my sister and her work clothing!

Its smell suffocated what fresh air had been in the chicken house, and a whole new situation arose for my sister, who had to be to work very soon. But what a story to tell, the story of the rotten eggs.

Anne LaBrake,
Custer

The Coming of Electricity

MY GRANDPARENTS, WILLIAM AND MABEL LEWIS, lived southwest of Newell on a 760-acre farm. It was a great place to visit as a child. We could and did have fun. The story that sticks out in my mind took place in the mid-1940s, when they received electricity.

They milked fifty head of Grade A Holstein cows and always had a few bum lambs. Grandma would have around one hundred New Hampshire Red chickens which produced thirty dozen eggs a week to sell between February and June to the Grandview Hatchery in Belle Fourche for hatching purposes. Then, during the off season, they would trade her surplus eggs for other groceries that were needed.

Electricity brought many changes, including milking machines, electric ranges, refrigerators, freezers, water heaters, and electric lights in the house and out buildings. It was nice to be able to walk out and see where you were going.

My grandparents lived a rather simple life. They did not have a radio or a television. They were a close knit family. They would play the piano or mandolin, and an accordion played by their daughters provided the family with musical entertainment. They enjoyed reading the Bible, and grandma was always working on a quilt for someone.

Betty Jo Huff,
Rural Newell

Teaching Myself to Sew During the Early 1940s

WORLD WAR II WAS IN FULL FORCE and many things were rationed. No one had very much money to spend. We were just married and had begun raising chickens and milking cows to make a living.

Feed for the baby chicks came in flowered feed sacks that could be used for making dresses, but I had never sewed much and we didn't even have a sewing machine. A kind neighbor lady who was losing her eyesight and could not sew anymore offered me an old Homestead brand peddle-type sewing machine for five dollars. My husband always said that was the best five dollars he ever spent.

Friends had given me old clothes to make over into clothes for my kids. My first attempt was to take a pink wool ladies coat and make it into a coat for our first daughter when she was one. I know there were some mistakes, but it fit her fine and she was warm. I used scraps to make quilts for our beds. I recall a man's suit which was given to us. I made my own patterns and made a western style suit for our little boy. It fit him so nice that his Dad bought him a cowboy hat to go with his suit.

We finally got to the point where I could buy yard goods to make clothes. Our two older girls belonged to a 4-H sewing club. They both learned to sew and made many of their own clothes when they were in high school. I made patterns for western shirts and made the shirts from new material for them. One of my favorite patterns was for a princess style dress, which was popular in the sixties. I made many of these for my youngest three girls and my granddaughters. In the sixties, I always sewed pajamas for my young girls and grandkids each year for Christmas gifts. This required many long hours of sewing into the wee hours of the night as I didn't have time to sew until late at night.

Della Studt,
Rural Presho

Home Brew

DAD USED TO MAKE HOME-BREW BEER. It aged in an outside cellar till it was ready to drink. Dad made quite a few trips out there for sampling before the beer was really ready. Then he and Mom would butcher a beef and a hog. There was no such thing as refrigeration in those days, so the meat still had to be processed for keeping. The head, heart, and tongue were used in headcheese. Some fresh meat was hung when it was cold. It was usually winter anyway. A lot of the meat was cooked and canned. The rest was usually smoked, such as hams and wuess (baloney).

Later in the year the weather was warm enough to take a wagon and team to Vivian, five miles away. When we came home, the cellar door was open, which upset Dad some. But all hell broke loose when he heard talk and laughter and discovered two or three neighbors down there drinking his home brew and eating his wuess. I had never heard Dad angry with other people before, but he finally cooled down and then sat down with the intruders. They started talking and laughing again, as Dad came up with some of his favorite German songs. He also told them they could come back anytime as long as they asked. Just don't ever party without him.

Robert F. Gloe,
Lyman County
Submitted By Dianne R. Gloe

Suggestions for Further Research, Thought, and Discussion

1. Locate old photographs of farms and ranches in your community and talk to people about the buildings and equipment they had on their properties. Draw diagrams of the houses, barns, outbuildings, and farmyards of these places.

2. Obtain old newspapers on microfilm and trace the trajectories of prices for livestock and crops over time. Look for old financial records of farm families showing both income and expenditures and compare them to current figures.

3. Get a county or community history book and read some of the family histories in it, looking for comments on weather events, farm machinery, social happenings, women's roles, diversions, and farm organizations.

4. Discuss the contrasting ways in which American Indians and white settlers thought about and treated the land.

5. Read a book on the history of American agriculture and compare the experience of living in South Dakota with general national trends.

6. Visit the Agricultural Heritage Museum in Brookings, the Cultural Heritage Center in Pierre, or other local and county museums and note how machinery, technology, and agricultural practices have changed over time.

7. Do a personal oral history project on one of the twelve themes highlighted in this book. Ask questions of people to fill in some of the gaps about how life has changed over the years on South Dakota farms and ranches.

8. Pick one of the twelve themes in this book and write your own story about personal experiences on the farm and ranch.

For Further Reading

Blasingame, Ike. *Dakota Cowboy: My Life in the Old Days.* New York: G. P. Putnam's Sons, 1958.

Conkin, Paul K. *A Revolution Down on the Farm: The Transformation of American Agriculture since 1929.* Lexington: University Press of Kentucky, 2008.

Danbom, David B. *Born in the Country: A History of Rural America.* 2d ed. Baltimore: Johns Hopkins University Press, 2006.

Fite, Gilbert C. *American Farmers: The New Minority.* Bloomington: Indiana University Press, 1981.

Gilfillan, Archer B. *Sheep: Life on the South Dakota Range.* 1929, reprint, St. Paul: Minnesota Historical Society Press, 1993.

Holden, David J. *Dakota Visions: A County Approach.* Sioux Falls: Center for Western Studies, 1982.

Hoover, Herbert T. "Farmers Fight Back: A Survey of Rural Political Organizations, 1873-1983." *South Dakota History* 13 (Spring/Summer 1983): 122-57.

Hurt, R. Douglas. *Indian Agriculture in America: Prehistory to the Present.* Lawrence: University Press of Kansas, 1996.

_____. *Problems of Plenty: The American Farmer in the Twentieth Century.* Chicago: Ivan R. Dee, 2002.

Janssen, Larry and Mark Edelman. *The Changing Structure of South Dakota Agriculture.* Brookings: SDSU Economics Department Research Report 83-2, January 1983.

Jennings, Dana Close. *Cattle on a Thousand Hills: A Story of Modern-Day Ranch Life: The Sutton Bros. of South Dakota.* Aberdeen: North Plains Press, 1968.

Jordan, Terry G. *North American Cattle-Ranching Frontiers: Origins, Diffusion, and Differentiation.* Albuquerque: University of New Mexico Press, 1993.

Knight, Richard L., Wendell C. Gilbert, and Ed Marston, eds. *Ranching West of the 100th Meridian: Culture, Ecology, and Economics.* Washington, D.C.: Island Press, 2002.

Latza, Greg. *Back on the Farm: Celebrating South Dakota Farm and Ranch Families.* Sioux Falls: PeopleScapes, Inc., 1999.

Lee, Bob. "Ranching: East to West." In Herbert T. Hoover, John E. Miller, et al. *A New South Dakota History.* Sioux Falls: Center for Western Studies, 2005: 255-87.

Lee, Bob and Dick Williams. *Last Grass Frontier: The South Dakota Stock Grower Heritage.* Sturgis: Black Hills Publishers, 1964.

Manfred, Frederick. *The Golden Bowl.* 1944, reprint, Albuquerque: University of New Mexico Press, 1980.

Nelson, Paula M. *The Prairie Winnows Out Its Own: The West River Country of South Dakota in the Years of Depression and Dust.* Iowa City: University of Iowa Press, 1996.

Oyos, Lynwood. "Farming: Dependency and Depopulation." In Herbert T. Hoover, John E. Miller, et al. *A New South Dakota History.* Sioux Falls: Center for Western Studies, 2005: 225-54.

Riley, Glenda. "Farm Women's Roles in the Agricultural Development of South Dakota." *South Dakota History* 13 (Spring/Summer 1983): 83-121.

Schell, Herbert S. and John E. Miller. *History of South Dakota.* 4th ed. Pierre: South Dakota State Historical Society Press, 2004.

Shover, John L. *First Majority, Last Minority: The Transforming of Rural Life in America.* DeKalb: Northern Illinois University Press, 1976.

Starrs, Paul F. *Let the Cowboy Ride: Cattle Ranching in the American West.* Baltimore: Johns Hopkins University Press, 1998.

Wagoner, Paula L. *"They Treated Us Just Like Indians": The Worlds of Bennett County, South Dakota.* Lincoln: University of Nebraska Press, 2002.

SOUTH DAKOTA HUMANITIES COUNCIL

The South Dakota Humanities Council (SDHC), founded in 1972 in response to an act of Congress, is the only cultural organization in the state whose sole mission is to deliver humanities programming to the people of South Dakota. As a steward of the state's cultural awareness and heritage, the Council cultivates statewide interest in South Dakota history, literature and other related humanities subjects, while stimulating an interest in the state's place as part of the universal human experience. This programming vision forms the core mission of SDHC—"to support and promote the exchange of ideas to foster a thoughtful and engaged society." The staff and board of directors of SDHC envision a South Dakota:

• Where we fulfill our essential human need to tell our stories, satisfy our curiosity, and take action in response to our vision of a better world.

• Where we have the tools we need to participate fully in the cultural and civic life of our communities.

• Where we celebrate the tapestry of life, family and place that make South Dakota unique and unifies us in our diversity.

The agency supports and promotes humanities public programming and grant funding to South Dakota non-profit and educational organizations. These include:

Financial Grant Support: Available for community organizations through Humanities Discussion, Media, and Research grants. Also, $15,000 is set aside to fund a Teachers' Institute for Native Americans.

South Dakota Center for the Book: A part of SDHC since 2002, it houses community reading programs including "One Book South Dakota," an annual Festival of Books, the youth reflective writing program "Letters about Literature," a pilot project "Literature and Medicine," as well as authorship and research opportunities.

Speakers' Bureau Program: Provides funding for humanities scholars to present on various topics throughout South Dakota. An annual catalog features over nearly 60 presenters with more than 80 unique presentations, including Chautauqua-style characterizations. With this program, $5,000 is set aside in perpetuity specifically for American Indian cultural programs. Programs are encouraged on or near reservations.

Museum on Main Street: Offers Smithsonian exhibits to rural communities in our state. The exhibition "Between Fences" traveled to six communities in 2008-2009, and a new exhibit will be chosen for the 2011 program year.

Resource Center: Includes a lending library of two in-house traveling exhibits as well as exhibits from the South Dakota Historical Society through the Cultural Heritage Center.

Civic Education Programs: SDHC supports "We the People," a civic education curriculum, and "History Day," a competition coordinated by the South Dakota Agricultural Heritage Museum.

Our mission is made possible by you! If you would like to donate to help fund these programs, please consider one of the following options:

Online: Visit our website at www.sdhumanities.org and donate securely via PayPal.

Mail: Send a check payable to SDHC at 1215 Trail Ridge Road, Suite A, Brookings, SD 57006
Phone: Call our office at 605/688-6113.
For more information, please call, visit our website, or email us at info@sdhumanities.org.

SOUTH DAKOTA STORIES
from
South Dakota Humanities Council

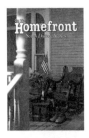

ON THE HOMEFRONT, the latest in the series, is a collection of stories contributed by people from across South Dakota, you will explore not only perspectives of those who served on the front line, but you will also share in the experiences of those left to defend another front. The Homefront.
Edited by Dr. Charles Woodard

COUNTRY CONGREGATIONS highlights the experiences and perspectives shared by members of rural religious communities, including those of tribal people, across South Dakota.

Edited by Dr. Charles Woodard

ONE-ROOM COUNTRY SCHOOL contains 145 stories from South Dakota contributors and former residents reflecting on their experiences in one-room country schools.

Edited by Dr. Norma Wilson & Dr. Charles Woodard